Easy Artisan

Simple, Elegant Recipes for the Everyday Cook

Anne K. Baldzikowski
with Illustrations by Mary Fordham Kuckens

Copyright © 2014
Anne Baldzikowski
All Rights Reserved

No part of this publication may be reproduced, distributed, or transmitted in any form or by any means, including photocopying, recording, or other electronic or mechanical methods, without the prior written permission of the publisher, except in the case of brief quotations embodied in critical reviews and certain other noncommercial uses permitted by copyright law. For permission requests, write to the publisher at the address below.

Published by

Flower Cottage Press
P.O. Box 1176
Capitola, Ca 95010

Printed in the United States of America
1st Edition
ISBN 978-0-9909521-0-7

14 13 12 11 10 / 10 9 8 7 6 5 4 3 2 1

Cover and Author Photos by: Jeanne Baldzikowski

Dedicated to my students whose enthusiasm and creativity I am so grateful for.

APPETIZERS 1

Pesto Cheese Torta 3
Fresh Berry Salsa 4
Salsa Fresca 4
Salami Pinwheels 5
Parmesan Cheese Straws 6
Rice Paper Wraps 7
Inari Sushi 8
Mini Vegetable Quiche 9
Herb and Cheese Cream Scones 10
Cherry Tomato Crostini 11

BREAKFAST 13

Apple Coffee Cake 15
Gluten-Free Banana Coffee Cake 16
Gluten-Free Pumpkin Coffee Cake 17
Bacon and Cheese Scones 18
Chocolate Scones 19
Henny Penny Egg 20
Chocolate Banana Strudel 21
Hearty Steel Cut Oatmeal 22
Green Smoothie 23

SOUPS 25

Black Bean Soup 27
Cream of Broccoli Soup 28
Garden Fresh Tomato Soup 29
Italian Sausage Soup 30
Leek and Potato Soup 31
Cassoulet Soup 32

SIDE DISHES 33

Coconut Rice 35
Couscous 36
Garlic Mashed Potatoes 37
Polenta 38
Tian 39
Summer Gratin 40
Pasta Alfredo 41
Lemon Basil Pasta 42
Quinoa 43
Corn Bread with Honey Butter 44

ENTREES 45

Cheesy Pesto Tart 47
Cocoa Carne Asada 48
Teriyaki Salmon 49
Salmon Sliders with Wasabi Mayonnaise 50
Chicken Molé 51
Tomato Basil Galette 52
Black Bean Chili con Carne 53
Sushi 54

DESSERTS 57

Plum Crisp 59
Matt's Apple Crisp 60
Strawberry Rhubarb Cobbler 61
Apple Pocket Pies 62
Dana's Blueberry Buckle 63

COOKIES 65

Meyer Lemon Refrigerator Cookies 67
Cacao Nib Butter Cookies 68
Peanut Butter Gems 69
Oatmeal Cookies 70
Cantuccini 71
Gluten-Free Flour Blend 71
Bountiful Jam Squares 72
Gluten-Free Bountiful Jam Squares 73

CAKES 75

Apple Spice Cake with Cream Cheese Icing 77
Simple Plum Cake 78
Glamorous French Chocolate Cake 79
Jeanne's Strawberry Shortcake 80

GALETTES & TARTS 83

Galette Pastry Dough 85
Very Berry Galette 86
Streusel Topping 86
Fruit Galette Variations: Blackberry, Pear, Apple, Nectarine, Plum, Apricot 87
Pumpkin Chiffon Tart 88
Southern Pecan Tart with Cinnamon Whipped Cream 89
Tart Dough 90
Chocolate Walnut Tart 90
Fresh Fruit Tart 91

ICE CREAM, SORBET & SAUCES 93

Vanilla Ice Cream 95
Mexican Chocolate Ice Cream 96
Fresh Strawberry Sorbet 97
Chocolate Sauce 98
Caramel Sauce 99
Ice Cream Cones, Cups, and Fortune Cookies 100

CONFECTIONS 103

Chocolate Peanut Clusters 105
Aztec Truffles 106
Lollipops 107
Rocky Road Candy 108
Almond Brittle 109
Pâte de Fruit 110

October 11, 2014

Today I taught class to a group of novice cooks. When I began to explain how to use fillo dough, a look of horror flashed over a few of the students' faces. I didn't want anyone running out of the classroom, so I gently encouraged them that the dough was fairly easy to work with following my techniques and that they would enjoy using it in the bakeshop. Really!

A few minor blips occurred during the course of the class, but with encouraging words and a light attitude, people relaxed and were soon busily chatting away and preparing delicious homemade treats. With quality ingredients prepared in small batches, my students embraced the essence of artisan cuisine.

When preparing food for my family and teaching culinary classes, I like to take the next step to make artisan cooking easy. Sure you can spend four days making a loaf of bread, but why not take the same high quality ingredients, use a simpler approach, and end up with a delicious product sooner.

Join me on this artisan journey as I share my well-tested recipes and techniques that have brought pleasure to many. Along the way you will see my sister Mary's lovely illustrations of the dishes made from this book.

I believe that through using food as an art medium we can create beauty and cultivate an inner joy and appreciation for our lives. After all, life is given meaning through everyday pleasures and eating is something we do every day. Why not create simple beautiful food and share it with others as an expression of gratitude.

With this book I hope to share my experience with readers to begin or extend the cultivation of their own artisanal cooking experiences.

In my 14 years of teaching culinary arts professionally I have encouraged thousands of people to cultivate their inner chef. My easy artisanal recipes work in a friendly format and have been inspired and tested by many students. With this book I hope to reach and inspire an even broader range of food lovers and to share my recipes and techniques.

Express your inner artisan with joy,
Anne Baldzikowski

A Few Guidelines Before You Begin...

Here are a few tips for you to follow when making the recipes.

- ~ It's always a good idea to read the recipe from beginning to end, making sure you have all the ingredients, necessary equipment and understand the directions before you begin.
- ~ all eggs are large
- ~ all butter is salted unless otherwise specified
- ~ all salt is kosher
- ~ all pepper is freshly ground black pepper unless otherwise specified
- ~ all herbs and spices are dried unless otherwise specified
- ~ all milk is whole
- ~ all temperatures are Fahrenheit

Appetizers

Appetizers

Pesto Cheese Torta

Fresh Berry Salsa

Salsa Fresca

Salami Pinwheels

Parmesan Cheese Straws

Rice Paper Wraps

Inari Sushi

Mini Vegetable Quiche

Herb and Cheese Cream Scones

Cherry Tomato Crostini

Pesto Cheese Torta

Creamy cheese and zesty pesto layered in a colorful mound accents any appetizer buffet. You can serve this with freshly cut vegetables, crackers, flatbreads, fresh or toasted baguette rounds. For parties I like to make an array of appetizers arranged on a side table. It's always a good idea to serve a few appetizers that keep guests busy and this is one of them.

MAKES ONE TORTA

Ingredients

3/4 cup, pesto (see recipe below)

At room temperature:
1 pound cream cheese
4 ounces unsalted butter
4 ounces mascarpone cheese

Pesto (Makes ¾ cup)

2 cups fresh basil leaves
2 cloves garlic, minced
2 tablespoons chopped walnuts, toasted
1/2 cup extra-virgin olive oil
1/4 teaspoon salt
1/8 teaspoon pepper
1/3 cup Parmesan cheese, grated

Place all of the ingredients in your blender and puree until smooth. Adjust seasonings and enjoy!

1. Line a round 4-cup bowl with plastic wrap.
2. Using a stand mixer with the whip attachment or food processor with the blade attachment, whip butter and cheeses until smooth.
3. Place one third of the cheese mixture in the bottom of your bowl, smoothing off the top.
4. Add one layer of pesto and repeat ending with the cheese mixture.
5. Wrap plastic up and over the top and place a heavy object (a jar of marinara) on top of the torta to weigh it down in the bowl.
6. Place in the refrigerator for at least an hour or up to 3 days.
7. To unmold the torta, remove the plastic wrap and turn the mold upside down on a platter.
8. Remove the plastic wrap and garnish with a basil spring. It is best eaten at room temperature.

Fresh Berry Salsa

Yes, strawberries and a splash of balsamic vinegar give a colorful take on our traditional Salsa Fresca (see below). A version of this recipe won my daughter Jeanne an award at our farmers market. My son also made points with his Spanish teacher, Ms. Murray, when I taught the students how to make this during a tostada party.

MAKES 4 CUPS

Ingredients

2 cups (4) Roma tomatoes diced
1 mango, diced
1 cup (6 medium) strawberries, diced
3 tablespoons (1/2 chili) Anaheim chili, seeded and minced
1/2 cup onion, diced
1/4 cup minced cilantro
1/2 teaspoon sea salt
3 tablespoons balsamic vinegar

Mix all ingredients in a bowl and adjust seasonings to taste. Add a bit more salt if it is bland or a bit more balsamic if it needs a tang. You can also replace the mild Anaheim chili with a jalapeño for a little heat.

Salsa Fresca

For a more traditional salsa try this recipe made with lots of fresh vegetables!

Makes 3 cups

Ingredients

6 medium tomatoes, diced
1/2 onion, diced
1/4 pepper, diced (try jalapeño for spicy or Anaheim for mild flavors)
1/2 lemon juiced
1 clove garlic, minced
1 cup cilantro, chopped
1/4 teaspoon salt
dash of pepper

Mix all ingredients in a bowl and adjust seasonings.

Salami Pinwheels

Before I started teaching at the college I was a substitute teacher at my children's elementary school during the week and made wedding cakes in my own business on the weekends. I loved sharing the joys of cooking with the children, but it was a challenge with no running water or stove in the classroom. We baked these French pastries in a toaster oven for my sister-in-law Jessica's first grade class.

MAKES 20 APPETIZERS

Ingredients

1 sheet (9 ounces) of store bought puff pastry dough, cold
1/4 cup all-purpose flour
4 tablespoons Dijon mustard
6 ounces salami, sliced
3 ounces (1 cup) mozzarella cheese, grated

1. If you are using frozen puff pastry defrost it in your refrigerator at least 4 hours before using. Preheat oven to 425 degrees. Line 2 cookie sheets with parchment paper and spray with pan spray. Lightly sprinkle your work table with flour and roll dough into a 12 by 12-inch square.
2. Brush dough with mustard. Cover mustard with salami rounds. Sprinkle with mozzarella cheese. Roll up pastry into a cylinder and slice into 1/2-inch rounds.
3. Place pinwheels onto parchment lined pans. Refrigerate for 15 minutes.
4. Bake for 8-10 minutes rotating your pans at about 6 minutes. Bake until pastries are golden brown. Serve warm.

Pesto Pinwheels Variation

Omit the salami and spread 4 ounces (7 tablespoons) pesto (page 3) on your square of pastry. Sprinkle 3 ounces (1cup) shredded mozzarella cheese on top, roll up, and proceed with the recipe.

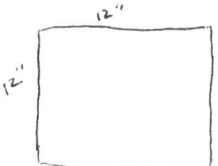
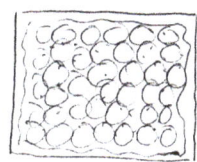

Parmesan Cheese Straws

Sure you can buy cheese straws at gourmet markets, but they will never be as fresh and crunchy as the ones you make. Place these in tall drinking glasses on your appetizer buffet near a plate of fresh veggies. A nibble of pastry then a few vegetables really balances out our pleasure center as well as our digestion.

MAKES 20-24

Ingredients

1 sheet (9 ounces) store bought puff pastry dough, cold

1 cup (3 ounces) Parmesan cheese, finely grated

Egg-wash

1 egg whisked with 1 tablespoon milk

1. If you are using frozen puff pastry defrost it in your refrigerator at least 4 hours before using. Preheat oven to 425 degrees. Line 2 cookie sheets with parchment paper and spray with pan spray. Lightly sprinkle your work table with 1/2 cup of the Parmesan cheese and roll dough into a 10 by 10-inch square.
2. Brush dough with egg-wash. Sprinkle with remaining Parmesan cheese. Press the cheese in with your palms.
3. Fold dough in half toward you and slice dough into 1/2-inch strips. Unfold strips and twist into spirals.
4. Place cheese twists onto greased parchment lined baking sheets. Refrigerate for 15 minutes.
5. Bake for 10-15 minutes rotating your pans at about 8 minutes. Bake until cheese straws are golden brown. Letting them sit on the pan, after baking, for 5 minutes before removing them makes it easier for the pastry to release from the parchment.

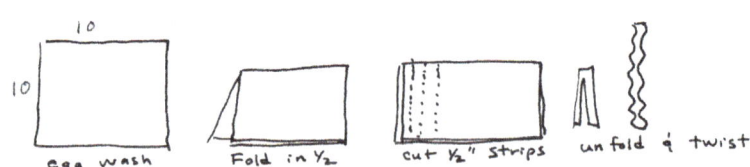

Rice Paper Wraps

Ingredients

Cucumber Rolls

10 eight-inch rice paper wrappers
3/4 cup mint leaves
3 medium carrots, shredded
1 English cucumber, peeled and sliced thin
8 lettuce leaves

Shrimp Rolls

10 eight-inch rice paper wrappers
8 lettuce leaves
1 English cucumber, peeled and sliced thin
3 medium carrots, shredded
3/4 cup cilantro leaves
8 medium shrimp, cooked and sliced in half

Dipping Sauce

1/4 cup peanut butter
1/2 cup sweet chili sauce
1/4 cup water
2 tablespoons hoisin sauce
2 teaspoons garlic, minced
2 teaspoons soy sauce

Mix all ingredients in a bowl. Adjust seasonings to taste.

Rice Noodles

3 ounces rice noodles
1 teaspoon salt
2 quarts water

These take a bit of time to prepare, but the rewards in beauty, flavor, and nutrition are ten-fold.

MAKES 10

You Will Need:

Rice paper wrappers (available at most grocery stores)
A bowl of warm water
Rice noodles, cooked
Ingredients for cucumber or shrimp rolls
Dipping Sauce

1. Bring the water with the salt to a boil in a 4-quart saucepan. Add the noodles and turn off the heat. Stir occasionally to prevent the noodles from sticking together.
2. Let the noodles sit in the hot water for about 10 minutes until they are tender and opaque (no longer clear). You can bite into a noodle to test for doneness.
3. Rinse the noodles in cold water, drain, and set aside.

To Wrap the Rolls

1. Have a bowl of warm (100 degrees) water on your work surface.
2. Dip the wrapper in the water for about 10 seconds, until just soft.
3. Lay the wrapper on a plate and let rest 15 seconds to absorb the water.
4. Lay the fillings on the bottom third of the wrapper.
5. Roll one third of the wrapper away from you, tuck in the sides, and continue rolling until the ends meet. With the seam on the bottom, slice cylinder in half at an angle. Keep the filled wraps under a damp towel until ready to eat.
6. Serve with dipping sauce.

Inari Sushi

At our local Hawaiian restaurant these are called cone sushi. Young people especially love these sweet pockets of seasoned tofu stuffed with moist rice. During the summer the college offers middle school and high school youth an array of classes. My week long cooking camps fill up quickly and this is a recipe that the kids love to make.

MAKES 8-10

Ingredients

1 cup sushi rice
2 cups water
1/2 teaspoon salt
1/4 cup rice vinegar
1 tablespoon sugar
1/2 teaspoon salt
1 can inarizushi-no-moto (seasoned fried bean curd available at gourmet shops or Asian markets)

Garnish

Sesame seeds
Sliced pickled ginger
Toasted chopped peanuts
Seaweed Gomasio, a dry mix of sea salt, sesame, and sea vegetables (available at natural food stores or Asian markets)

1. To remove the starch from the rice, rinse it with cold water, in a strainer, until the water is clear.
2. Place rice, water, and 1/2 teaspoon salt in a 4-quart sauce pan over high heat. Bring to a boil. Turn the heat down so the rice simmers and cover. It takes about 25-30 minutes to cook.
3. About 10 minutes before the rice finishes, when the water has just evaporated, turn off the heat. Remove the lid and place a towel over the pot and cover with the lid. This steams the rice and helps prevent mushy rice.
4. While rice is cooking, mix the rice vinegar, sugar, and 1/2 teaspoon salt together in a small pot or microwavable bowl and heat the ingredients until the sugar and salt are dissolved.
5. When rice is tender and water has evaporated, pour it into a shallow dish and pour the sweet vinegar over the rice stirring every 5 minutes or so until the rice stops steaming.
6. While rice is cooling open can of inarizushi-no-moto, and gently pull apart soy curd packets. Take a small handful of rice, about 1/4 cup, and fill the pockets. Sprinkle with your choice of garnish. Serve cold or at room temperature.

inari sushi

Mini Vegetable Quiche

I make these for my end-of-the-semester buffet. I walk into the classroom with a plate of these pastries fresh from the oven and always hear a few delighted sighs.

MAKES 24

Ingredients

3 tablespoons butter
1/2 cup red onion, diced
Salt and pepper, to taste
Cayenne, pinch
1 can (8.5 ounces) artichokes, chopped
2 eggs
2 cups (6 ounces) grated Parmesan and Swiss cheese
4 ounces cream
18 ounces puff pastry dough, cold

1. If you are using frozen puff pastry defrost it in your refrigerator at least 4 hours before using. Preheat oven to 425 degrees. Lightly grease mini muffin tins.
2. Roll out pastry to 1/8-inch thick. Cut out 3-inch rounds with a pastry cutter. Place rounds in the tins, poke holes all over the bottom of pastry with a fork (docking), and chill 15 minutes.
3. In a sauté pan, heat butter until it bubbles, add onion and cook until tender. Add artichokes and heat through. Season with salt, pepper, and the Cayenne.
4. In a separate bowl, whisk together the eggs, cheese, and cream. Combine with the vegetable mixture.
5. Fill pastry shells with one heaping tablespoon of filling. Bake 10-12 minutes at 425 degrees.

Variation

Place pastry in tins, dock, fill, and freeze with uncooked filling. When frozen, pop out of tins and place in freezer bags. Freeze one month. When ready to cook, pop quiches back in muffin tins and bake 20-25 minutes at 425 degrees.

Herb & Cheese Cream Scones

I enjoy growing my own thyme and chives in pots in a sunny area on the patio. These delicious colorful scones are perfect on an appetizer buffet or served alongside a bowl of soup Leek and Potato Soup (page 31).

MAKES 12 SCONES

Ingredients

2 cups all-purpose flour
2 ½ teaspoons baking powder
1/2 teaspoon salt
1 tablespoon, chopped fresh thyme
2 tablespoons chopped fresh chives
1 1/8 cups (4 ounces) cheddar cheese, shredded
1 1/4 cups heavy cream

Garnish

1 tablespoon heavy cream
1 tablespoon poppy seeds

1. Preheat oven to 400 degrees.
2. Line a cookie sheet with parchment paper. Draw an 8-inch circle on the parchment and flip the parchment over with the pen side facing down. Spray your parchment with pan spray.
3. In a medium sized bowl, sift together flour, sugar, baking powder, and salt. Stir in the herbs and shredded cheese.
4. Make a well in the center of the dry ingredients and pour in the 1 ¼ cups cream. Stir the mixture with a large spatula pressing down the dough along the sides of the bowl to moisten all of the dry ingredients. The dough will look a little lumpy.
5. Knead the dough in your bowl until it comes together. Scoop the dough out onto your 8-inch template and shape into a circle.
6. Cut the circle into 12 triangles. Work quickly because you do not want the dough to become warm, the scones will not rise as high.
7. Arrange the scones onto your parchment lined cookie sheet and brush with remaining 1 tablespoon cream and sprinkle with poppy seeds. Bake for 15-17 minutes or until tops are golden brown.

Cherry Tomato Crostini

Roasting cherry tomatoes condenses the flavor and makes them easy to bite into without the seeds and juice popping out. In July I lead a group of students across campus to the farmers market, where we meet with local farmers who delight us with tomato folklore and many tastings. We fill our baskets with the love apples and head back to the classroom to create. These crostini are colorful to the eyes and bursting with flavor.

MAKES 14-16

Ingredients

1 pound cherry tomatoes, use a variety for a rainbow of color
1 tablespoon olive oil
1/4 teaspoon kosher salt
A few twists of freshly ground pepper
3 sprigs oregano or thyme

Crostini (toasted bread slices)

1/2 baguette, sliced into 1/2-inch rounds
1/3 cup extra-virgin olive oil

Ricotta Topping

Mix 1 cup ricotta cheese seasoned with 1/4 teaspoon salt and fresh ground pepper.

Garnish

1/4 cup extra-virgin olive oil
Coarse salt
Fresh ground pepper

1. Preheat oven to 350 degrees.
2. Line a baking pan with parchment paper. Place the tomatoes onto the parchment and drizzle with olive oil. Season with salt, pepper, and oregano leaves.
3. Roast tomatoes for 45 minutes, until they burst and the edges caramelize just a bit.
4. While tomatoes are roasting, brush olive oil on one side of sliced baguette rounds.
5. Place the rounds oiled side down on a parchment lined baking sheet and toast for 7-10 minutes.

To Prepare the Crostini

1. Take a slice of bread, toasted side up, and spread on a thick layer of ricotta topping.
2. Top with a few cherry tomatoes, drizzle with olive oil, sprinkle on coarse salt, and fresh ground pepper. Enjoy!

Breakfast

Apple Coffee Cake

Gluten-Free Banana Coffee Cake

Gluten-Free Pumpkin Coffee Cake

Bacon and Cheese Scones

Chocolate Scones

Henny Penny Egg

Chocolate Banana Strudel

Hearty Steel Cut Oatmeal

Green Smoothie

Apple Coffee Cake

Here's a coffee cake that comes together easily and can be made with just about any fruit or vegetable you have around your home depending upon the season or what is in your fruit basket.

SERVES 12

Ingredients

1 ½ cups all-purpose flour
1/4 teaspoon salt
2 teaspoons cinnamon
1 cup coconut sugar, or granulated sugar
1/4 teaspoon baking soda
1 teaspoon baking powder
2 small apples, cored and cut into small pieces
1/3 cup olive oil
1 egg, beaten
1 cup buttermilk
1/4 cup oats
2 tablespoons turbinado sugar or granulated sugar

1. Preheat the oven to 350 degrees. Spray a 13 by 9-inch baking dish, with cooking spray.
2. In a large bowl, sift together the flour, salt, cinnamon, sugar, baking soda, and baking powder.
3. Add chopped apples to dry ingredients.
4. In a medium-sized bowl whisk together the olive oil, egg, and buttermilk.
5. Make a well in the center of the dry ingredients and pour in the wet ingredients. Fold mixture gently with a spatula.
6. Pour batter into prepared pan. Sprinkle top with oats and turbinado sugar.
7. Bake for 30 minutes or until a toothpick inserted in the center comes out clean.

Variations

If using pieces of fruit, use about 2 cups: pears, peaches, blueberries, or other chopped fruits.

If using wet fruit or vegetables, use one cup: banana, pumpkin puree, shredded zucchini or other wet fruits.

Gluten-Free Banana Coffee Cake

We always seem to have bananas in the house. They are the perfect snack on the go, or pureed in smoothies. They also have the perfect sweetness and texture for baking.

SERVES 8-10

Ingredients

1 ½ cups gluten-free flour blend (page 71)

1/4 teaspoon salt

2 teaspoons cinnamon

1 cup coconut sugar, or granulated sugar

1/4 teaspoon baking soda

1 teaspoon baking powder

2 bananas sliced, about 2 cups

1/3 cup olive oil

1 egg, beaten

1 cup buttermilk

1/4 cup oats

2 tablespoons turbinado sugar or granulated sugar

1. Preheat the oven to 350 degrees and spray a 1/4 sheet pan or an 8 by 12-inch baking dish with cooking spray.
2. In a large bowl, sift together the flour, salt, cinnamon, sugar, baking soda, and baking powder.
3. In a medium-sized bowl, whisk together the olive oil, egg, and buttermilk.
4. Make a well in the center of the dry ingredients and pour in the wet ingredients. Whisk the mixture until all the ingredients are combined.
5. Pour batter into prepared pan. Sprinkle top with the sliced bananas, oats and turbinado sugar. Let the batter sit in the pan 10 minutes, so the grains in the flour are moistened.
6. Bake for 25-30 minutes or until a toothpick inserted in the center comes out clean.

Gluten-Free Pumpkin Coffee Cake

Here is another tasty variation of my coffee cake for our gluten-free friends.

SERVES 8-10

Ingredients

1 ½ cups cups gluten-free flour blend (page 71)
1/4 teaspoon salt
2 teaspoons cinnamon
1 cup coconut sugar, or granulated sugar
1/4 teaspoon baking soda
1 teaspoon baking powder
1/3 cup olive oil
1 egg, beaten
1 cup buttermilk
1 cup canned pumpkin puree
1/2 cup raisins
1/2 cup pecans, chopped
1/4 cup oats
2 tablespoons turbinado sugar, or granulated sugar

1. Preheat the oven to 350 degrees and spray a ¼ sheet pan or an 8 by 12-inch pan with cooking spray.
2. In a large bowl sift together the flour, salt, cinnamon, sugar, baking soda, and baking powder.
3. In a medium-sized bowl, whisk together the olive oil, egg, buttermilk, and pumpkin puree.
4. Make a well in the center of the dry ingredients and pour in the wet ingredients. Whisk until just combined. Fold in the raisins with a spatula.
5. Pour batter into greased pan. Sprinkle top with pecans, oats, and turbinado sugar.
6. Bake for 25-30 minutes or until a toothpick inserted in the center comes out clean.

Bacon & Cheese Scones

Bacon is a family favorite around here. In moderation of course! Serve these at a special breakfast or with a bowl of Cassoulet Soup (page 32).

MAKES 16

Ingredients

2 cups all-purpose flour
2 teaspoons sugar
1/4 teaspoon salt
1 tablespoon baking powder
4 ounces butter, cold and cut into tablespoon-sized pieces
4 ounces (1 1/8 cups) sharp cheddar cheese, shredded
4-5 slices thick-cut bacon cooked and chopped
1 cup heavy cream, cold
1 egg, cold
1 tablespoon chives, chopped
All-purpose flour for dusting

Garnish

1 tablespoon poppy seeds
2 tablespoons heavy cream

1. Preheat oven to 400 degrees and line a cookie sheet with parchment paper. Draw two, 8-inch circles on the parchment and flip the parchment over with the pen side down. Spray the paper with pan spray.
2. Mix together the dry ingredients: flour, sugar, salt, and baking powder.
3. Rub the butter into the dry ingredients, with your fingers, until mixture has the texture of marbles, peas, and corn meal. Stir in the cheese, bacon, and chives.
4. In another bowl, mix together the egg and cream.
5. Make a well in the center of the dry ingredients and pour in the wet ingredients. Mix with a spatula until ingredients are just moistened.
6. Scrape mixture out of bowl onto a lightly floured table.
7. Knead dough 10-12 times until all ingredients are incorporated. Work quickly because you do not want the dough to become warm, the scones will not rise as high.
8. Divide the dough in half and pat the dough onto your 8-inch templates. Cut each dough circle into 8 triangles. Arrange scones on your parchment lined pan. They will be close together.
9. Brush scones with cream and sprinkle with poppy seeds.

Chocolate Scones

We like to bake these when we have overnight guests. Waking up to the aroma of coffee and chocolate makes everyone smile when they walk into our kitchen!

MAKES 12

Ingredients

2 cups all-purpose flour
2 teaspoons sugar
1 tablespoon baking powder
1/4 teaspoon salt
4 ounces butter, cold cut into tablespoon-sized pieces
4 ounces semisweet chocolate, chopped or chocolate chips
1 egg, cold
3/4 cups heavy cream, cold

Garnish

1 tablespoon heavy cream
1 tablespoon turbinado sugar, or granulated sugar

1. Preheat oven to 400 degrees. Line a cookie sheet with parchment paper. Draw two, 8-inch circles on the parchment and flip the parchment over with the pen side down. Spray with pan spray.
2. Mix together the dry ingredients: flour, sugar, salt, and baking powder.
3. Rub the butter into the dry ingredients, with your fingers, until mixture has the texture of marbles, peas, and cornmeal.
4. Stir in the chocolate pieces.
5. In another bowl, mix together the egg and heavy cream.
6. Make a well in the center of the dry ingredients and pour in the wet ingredients.
7. Mix with a spatula until ingredients are just moistened and scrape mixture out of the bowl onto the cookie sheet lined with parchment.
8. Knead with a dough scraper 10-12 times until all ingredients are incorporated.
9. Cut dough into two pieces. Shape into two disks about 8" round and cut each disk into 6 triangles.
10. Brush tops with cream and sprinkle with turbinado sugar. Bake for 10 minutes, rotate your pan, and bake another 10 minutes, until tops are golden brown.

Henny Penny Egg

Henny Penny was our beloved chicken who gave us beautiful mahogany colored eggs. This is a delicious breakfast that you can eat on the go or at your leisure. One thing is for sure: this breakfast is quick to prepare, light on the digestion, and nutritious enough to last until lunchtime.

MAKES 1

Ingredients

1 egg
1 teaspoon olive oil
1 slice whole grain bread
salt and pepper

1. Place a small, 8-inch sauté pan onto your stove top and turn heat on medium high. Add oil, salt, and pepper.
2. When oil shimmers crack egg into center of pan, breaking yolk.
3. Turn down heat to low. Take the slice of bread and tear out a 2-3-inch hole or so in the center of the bread. Eat or discard removed bread piece.
4. Place bread over egg with the center hole right over the center of the egg.
5. Cook about 2 minutes.
6. Flip egg with bread with a spatula and cook another 2 minutes or until the egg is done to your liking.

Chocolate Banana Strudel

Strudel is a German word meaning whirlwind. This delicious pastry is a long rectangular shape made of many layers of paper-thin dough. We use phyllo or fillo dough. Both are interchangeable and readily available in the freezer section of your grocery store. Chocolate and banana is a classic combination, one the students are very happy to prepare!

MAKES 6-8 SERVINGS

Ingredients

5 sheets phyllo dough, defrosted overnight in the refrigerator

5 tablespoons of butter, melted

3 bananas, sliced

1/4 cup sugar, plus 3 tablespoons

1/4 teaspoon cinnamon

3 ounces semisweet chocolate, chopped (or 1/2 cup chocolate chips)

1. Set the oven temperature to 475 degrees. Line a cookie sheet with parchment paper.
2. Remove phyllo from the refrigerator, unwrap, and cover with a dry towel.
3. In a small bowl, combine the bananas, 1/4 cup sugar, cinnamon, and chocolate. Now you are ready to assemble the strudel.
4. Place one sheet of phyllo on the parchment-lined pan. Gently brush with melted butter. Sprinkle with 1 teaspoon of sugar. Repeat four more times.
5. Place banana chocolate mixture down the center of the stack of phyllo sheets leaving a 2-inch border around the sides and 2 ½-inches from the top and bottom.
6. Fold in the sides of the phyllo, then gently roll and fold the strudel away from you. Finish with the seam side down.
7. Brush with remaining butter and sprinkle with remaining sugar.
8. Make four 2-inch vents down the center of the strudel and bake for 15 minutes. Cool for 15-20 minutes and serve.

 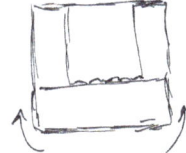 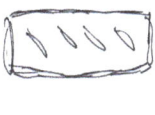

Hearty Steel Cut Oatmeal

For those mornings when your body craves grains, this a good breakfast to have waiting in the fridge. Warm it up in a pot or microwave and add colorful dried fruits and protein rich nuts.

MAKES 5 CUPS

Ingredients

4 cups water
1 cup steel-cut oats

1. Place water and oats in a four-quart saucepan. Turn the heat on high and bring to a boil stirring occasionally.
2. Once the mixture boils turn off the heat, cover, and let sit overnight at room temperature, no more than 12 hours, or the oats discolor.
3. In the morning, stir in one more cup of water. Place the pot back on the stove. Cook on a medium high heat stirring occasionally. When the oatmeal boils, lower the heat to a simmer.
4. Simmer for 10 minutes, stirring occasionally.
5. Remove from heat and scoop out the oatmeal that you plan to eat right away. Cool the remaining oatmeal on the counter for a few hours and then place in glass containers. I usually put some in the refrigerator and some in the freezer. Keeps one week in the refrigerator and 2 months in the freezer.

Toppings

Coconut sugar
Chia seeds
Flax seeds
Unsweetened coconut
Physillium husk
Your favorite dried fruit

Green Smoothie

After teaching a night of French pastry making I often whip up one of these smoothies up in the morning to balance out the rich pastry I indulged in the night before. My family is happy to start their day off with a glassful of goodness also.

MAKES TWO PINTS

Ingredients

1 large handful of kale, (we grow this year round)
1 cup frozen fruit, try mango, strawberries or blueberries
1 banana, peeled
1 apple, cored and chopped
1 orange, peeled
1 cup almond milk
1/2 cup water
1 tablespoon chia seeds
1 tablespoon flax meal
1 tablespoon Phsyllium husk

1. Place all ingredients in your blender and puree until really smooth. I usually get complaints if there are chunks! Add more liquid as needed. Feel free to replace any of the ingredients to your liking.

Soups

Black Bean

Cream of Broccoli

Garden Fresh Tomato

Italian Sausage

Leek and Potato

Cassoulet

Black Bean Soup

Soups can be prepared in a wide variety of ways, from delicate to hearty. This soup falls in the hearty category. With 15 grams of protein per cup of beans it falls in the healthy category as well. Enjoy!

SERVES 6-8

Ingredients

1 tablespoon olive oil
2 medium onions, diced
3 cloves garlic, minced
2 teaspoons chili powder
1 teaspoon unsweetened cocoa powder
3 cups (two, 15 ounce cans drained) cooked black beans (see below for recipe on how to cook black beans)
4 cups water or chicken, beef, or vegetable stock
1/4 - 1/2 teaspoon salt
1/8 teaspoon pepper
1/4 teaspoon red pepper flakes
Fresh lime juice, sour cream, and minced cilantro to garnish

1. Heat the oil in a stock pot. When it shimmers, add onions and cook until softened over medium heat. This takes 8-10 minutes.
2. Stir in the garlic and chili powder and cook for about a minute.
3. Add cocoa powder, beans, stock, salt, and pepper. Bring to a boil.
4. Reduce heat and simmer 10 minutes. Ladle half of the soup into your blender and puree, then pour back into your pot of soup and adjust seasonings.
5. Ladle into warm bowls and garnish with sour cream, cilantro, and a squeeze a bit of lime.

Variations on Bean Soup

Add any bits of smoked meats such as ham or bacon.
Add precooked vegetables or jalapeños.
Garnish with croutons, fresh chopped tomatoes, or fresh minced herbs.

Cooking Dry Black Beans: Two Different Methods

1. Fill a pot with cold water. Add 2 cups (1 pound) of beans and let sit on the counter overnight. Drain the water. Add 5 cups fresh water to cover the beans by an inch. Add 1/2 teaspoon salt, 2 tablespoons olive oil, 3 bay leaves and 3 cloves garlic smashed. Bring to a boil and then simmer 45 minutes to 1 hour, stirring occasionally. Skim the foam off the surface. Beans should remain below the surface of the water. Taste 5 beans for doneness. They should have a creamy texture. Eat within 3 days.

2. Place 2 cups (one pound) beans and 5 cups water in a stock pot. Turn heat on high and bring to a boil. Skim the foam off of the top. Reduce the heat to low so that the beans are simmering. Add 1/2 teaspoon salt, 2 tablespoons olive oil, 3 bay leaves, and 3 cloves garlic smashed and cover for 1 to 1 1/2 hours, stirring occasionally. Beans should remain below the surface of the water. Taste 5 beans for doneness. Eat within 3 days.

Cream of Broccoli Soup

This is a favorite wintertime soup at our house. As a child I once visited my Great Aunt Norma, where she worked in the office, at a Castroville packing shed. The workers were all busily packaging broccoli. The aroma was quite pungent!

SERVES 8-10

Ingredients

1/4 cup olive oil
2 medium onions, diced
2 cloves garlic, minced
2 pounds broccoli, cut into bite-sized pieces
1 russet potato, peeled and cut into bite-sized pieces
6 cups vegetable stock
1 pint heavy cream
1 teaspoon salt
1/8 teaspoon white pepper
1/4 cup minced chives

1. Heat oil in a stock pot. When it shimmers, add onions and cook until soft.
2. Add the broccoli pieces and stir to coat with the sautéed onions. Add the potatoes and the stock. Bring to a boil, then reduce the heat to a simmer and cook 20-30 minutes or until vegetables are tender.
3. Puree soup in 2 batches in your blender, pouring soup back into your stock pot after pureed.
4. Add the cream. Simmer 10-15 minutes. Adjust seasonings. Ladle soup in bowls and garnish with chives.

Garden Fresh Tomato Soup

Using a variety of tomatoes with this soup adds a unique color and highlights the amazing flavors of fresh garden tomatoes. Serve this soup with a wedge of Cornbread (page 44) and a dollop of Honey Butter (page 44).

SERVES 4-6

Ingredients

1/4 cup olive oil
1 large onion, chopped
2 cloves garlic, minced
1 large carrot, shredded
5 large tomatoes, cored and diced
10 basil leaves, cut into strips
3/4 teaspoon salt
1/8 teaspoon pepper
16 ounces chicken stock

Garnish

6 basil leaves

1. Heat the oil in a stock pot until it shimmers.
2. Sauté the onion, carrot and garlic until soft.
3. Add tomatoes, basil, seasonings, and stock.
4. Bring to a boil and then simmer for 10 minutes.
5. Puree the soup in your blender and adjust the seasonings.
6. Serve with a basil leaf garnish.

Italian Sausage Soup

Serve this hearty soup with Herb and Cheese Cream Scones (page 10) and you have a complete meal. Pump up your vitamins by substituting kale for the celery.

SERVES 8-10

Ingredients

1 pound Italian sausage, casings removed
2 onions, diced
4 cloves garlic, minced
2 cups (3 ribs) celery, diced
2 (15 ounce) cans diced tomatoes
2 (15 ounce) cans cannellini beans, rinsed
16 ounces chicken broth
1 cup dry white wine (I use Vermouth)

Garnish

1/3 cup grated Parmesan cheese

1. In a large stock pot, brown sausage over medium high heat.
2. Add onions and garlic and cook until soft.
3. Add celery and cook until soft.
4. Add the cans of tomatoes and beans.
5. Add the chicken broth and wine and turn heat to high, bringing soup to a boil.
6. Turn the heat down to a low simmer for 20 minutes.
7. Ladle into bowls and sprinkle with Parmesan cheese.

Leek & Potato Soup

Velvety smooth leek and potato soup is always a comfort on cold wintry days.

SERVES 8-10

Ingredients

1/4 cup olive oil
2 whole leeks, using only the white section, cut into 1/4-inch slices
1 1/2 pounds russet potatoes, peeled and quartered
32 ounces chicken stock, or vegetable stock
1 bay leaf
2 cups heavy cream
1/2 teaspoon salt
1/4 teaspoon white pepper
1/8 teaspoon nutmeg

Garnish

1/4 cup sour cream and 2 tablespoons milk whisked together and put in a squirt bottle.

1. Heat oil in a stock pot. When it shimmers add leek pieces and cook until tender.
2. Carefully pour the stock over the leeks. Add the potatoes, bay leaf, salt, pepper, and nutmeg.
3. Bring soup to a boil and then reduce heat to a simmer. Cook until the potatoes are tender.
4. Pull out the bay leaf and add cream.
5. Puree soup in 2 batches in your blender, pouring soup back into your stock pot after pureed.
6. Adjust seasonings. Ladle soup in bowls and squeeze a swirl of sour cream on top in a decorative pattern and serve.

Cassoulet Soup

Here is a soup created after the beloved white bean French stew, which often contains a variety of meats. The French stew, often presented with a layer of fat on top, is served in an earthenware container for cooking and serving. I add a bit more stock to make it the consistency of soup and keep the meats lean, so the layer of fat on top is minimal.

SERVES 8-10

Ingredients

- 1/4 cup olive oil
- 2 large onions, diced
- 9 cloves garlic, minced
- 4 ounce bacon, chopped
- 1 pound boneless chicken breast, cut in bite-sized pieces
- 1/4 teaspoon salt
- 1/8 teaspoon pepper
- 6 ounce tomato paste
- 3 cans pinto beans or white kidney beans
- 1/2 cup Vermouth
- 1 quart chicken stock
- 2 sprigs fresh thyme

1. Heat the oil, on medium-high heat, in large stock pot. When it shimmers, add onions and garlic. Cook until soft.
2. Add bacon and cook through.
3. Add chicken, salt, and pepper. Stir constantly until chicken is no longer pink.
4. Add tomato paste and cook for about five minutes, stirring constantly. The tomato paste will caramelize, adding more flavor to the soup.
5. Add beans, Vermouth, stock, and thyme.
6. Turn up heat to high and bring soup to a boil. Reduce heat and simmer for about 15 minutes. Adjust seasoning.
7. Serve in shallow bowls with French bread or Bacon and Cheese Scones (see page 18).

Side Dishes

Side Dishes

Coconut Rice

Couscous

Garlic Mashed Potatoes

Polenta

Tian

Summer Gratin

Pasta Alfredo

Lemon Basil Pasta

Quinoa

Corn Bread with Honey Butter

Coconut Rice

This is a lovely accompaniment to the Teriyaki Salmon (page 49).

MAKES 8 SERVINGS

Ingredients

2 cups jasmine or long grain rice
4 cups water
1/2 cup coconut, unsweetened
1 tablespoon extra-virgin olive oil
1/8 teaspoon black pepper
1 ½ teaspoons salt

1. To remove the starch from the rice, rinse it with cold water until the water is clear.
2. Place all ingredients in a 4-quart saucepan over high heat. Bring to a boil. Turn the heat down so the rice simmers then cover. It takes about 25-30 minutes to cook. You can also place all ingredients in a rice cooker and proceed with recipe.
3. About 10 minutes before the rice finishes, when the water has just evaporated, turn off the heat. Remove the lid and place a towel over the pot then cover with the lid. This steams the rice and helps prevent mushy rice.
4. When rice is cooked, let the rice sit 5 minutes with the lid on then fluff with a fork.

Couscous

This is easy to make and goes well with any entree that has a lot of sauce; the couscous will soak it up. Yum!

MAKES 8 SERVINGS

Ingredients

1 ½ cups water
2 tablespoons olive oil or butter
1/4 teaspoon salt
1 cup couscous

1. Pour water, olive oil, and salt into a 2-quart saucepan with a lid.
2. Cover the pot and bring the water to a boil on high heat
3. When water boils, remove pot from heat. Remove the lid and pour in the couscous.
4. Place pot back over high heat and bring to a boil.
5. Remove from heat. Let sit covered for 5 minutes.
6. Fluff with a fork, season with salt and pepper, and serve.

Garlic Mashed Potatoes

After reading Michael Pollan's research on potato farming, we eat only organic potatoes at the house. Freshly cooked organic russet potatoes combined with lots of garlic make a creamy side dish that disappears quickly.

SERVES 6-8

Ingredients

5 pounds russet potatoes, peeled and quartered
1 tablespoon salt
4 tablespoons butter
1 head of garlic, peeled and minced
1 cup milk, hot
1/2 teaspoon salt
1/8 teaspoon white pepper

1. Fill large pot with cold water and add potatoes and 1 tablespoon salt.
2. Bring potatoes to a boil with the lid off. Cook potatoes until tender. To test for doneness, take a potato out of the water and pierce it with a fork. If it slices easily, it is done. If it crumbles, it has cooked too long.
3. In a separate pan, heat the butter and garlic together over a very low heat for 5-10 minutes. Do not brown.
4. Drain potatoes in a colander, then transfer to a stand mixer. With the whip attachment whip potatoes for about 30 seconds. Scrape the bottom and sides of bowl and whip again for 30 seconds or until potatoes are lump free.
5. Add hot milk and garlic butter. Whip on low speed until all ingredients are thoroughly blended.
6. Season with the salt and white pepper.

Polenta

Placing some saucy meat or sautéed chicken on a spoonful of warm polenta is comfort food to my family. Try this with the Cocoa Carne Asada (page 48), or the Chicken Molé (page 51).

SERVINGS 4-6

Ingredients

4 cups water
1 teaspoon salt
1 cup polenta

1. Add water and salt to a 3-quart saucepan and cover with a lid.
2. Place over high heat and bring to a boil.
3. Remove lid from pot. Sprinkle in polenta and whisk to combine. Bring the polenta back up to a boil then reduce the heat to a simmer. Simmer 30 minutes, stirring occasionally with a wooden spoon. Stir in 1/4 to 1/2 cup of cheese at the end of the cooking time for richer flavor.

Variation

You may also pour the cooked polenta into a greased 9-inch spring-form pan. When the polenta cools, it sets up perfectly.

Slice the polenta in wedges. Place the wedges in a greased casserole dish and top individual pieces with marinara and mozzarella. Heat until cheese melts.

Tian

This is a French side dish that packs up easily for lunch or dinner at work. Most of my classes are 5-hours long with short breaks, so this is an easy snack to eat between rolling our pastries.

SERVES 9-12

Ingredients

1/2 tablespoon olive oil
2 cups cooked rice
1 tablespoon olive oil
2 cups chopped vegetables; such as zucchini, mushrooms, and carrots
1 clove garlic, minced
2 tablespoons fresh herbs, chopped; such as oregano and thyme
1/2 cup milk
4 eggs
1/2 cup Parmesan cheese or other hard cheese, shredded
1 slice bread, cut into small cubes, or 1/2 cup bread crumbs
Salt and pepper
1 tablespoon extra-virgin olive oil

1. Oil a 13 by 9-inch baking dish with ½ tablespoon olive oil and add the rice. Preheat oven to 350 degrees.
2. Pour 1 tablespoon oil in a sauté pan. Turn heat to medium high. When oil shimmers, add vegetables and cook until lightly brown. Add garlic and herbs. Cook another minute. Season with salt and pepper
3. Scoop the vegetables into the pan with the rice and toss. In a small bowl, mix eggs and milk with a little salt and pepper. Stir this into the rice mixture. Sprinkle with cheese and top with bread cubes. Drizzle with 1 tablespoon of olive oil.
4. Bake at 350 for 20 minutes or until firm. Cool and cut into squares.

Summer Gratin

The layering of bright red tomatoes, green zucchini, and creamy potatoes takes a little time, but the response from your family will be worth the effort when you bring your artwork to the table.

SERVES 9-12

Ingredients

2 tablespoons extra-virgin olive oil
2 large cloves garlic, minced
1 pound (about 5 or 6) medium to large tomatoes, sliced in 1/4-inch rounds
1 pound (one large 9 by 2-inches or so)) zucchini, sliced in 1/8-inch rounds
8 ounces (2) red potatoes, peeled and sliced in 1/8-inch rounds
1 teaspoon salt
1/4 teaspoon black pepper
1 tablespoon extra-virgin olive oil
Salt and pepper for seasoning
1 tablespoon fresh thyme
1/2 cup (2 ounces) strongly flavored shredded cheese (Parmesan and Swiss are good)

1. Preheat oven to 375 degrees. Drizzle the olive oil in a 13 by 9-inch baking dish. Sprinkle the chopped garlic evenly over the bottom of the pan and set aside.
2. Season the zucchini by placing sliced zucchini in a medium-sized bowl and tossing with 1 teaspoon salt and 1/4 teaspoon pepper.
3. Begin layering the sliced vegetables in a ring on the bottom of the seasoned baking dish, alternating a slice of tomato, potato, and then zucchini.
4. Once all of the vegetables are layered, drizzle with 1 tablespoon olive oil and season with salt and pepper. Top with grated cheese and thyme.
5. Cover baking dish with foil and bake for 35 minutes. Remove foil and bake another 35 minutes. The vegetables will be greatly reduced and tender. The cheese will be a little crispy around the edges.
6. Let sit 10 minutes and then slice and serve.

Pasta Alfredo

This pasta coated with a dreamy creamy sauce that originated in Rome is a big hit with teenagers that take my week-long summer cooking camps. They just keep going back to the Italian buffet and loading up their plates. Leftovers get taken home to lucky moms and dads.

SERVES 4-6

Ingredients

12 ounces pasta, fresh
1/4 cup (1/2 of a stick) of butter
1 ½ cups heavy cream
1/2 teaspoon pepper
1/8 teaspoon nutmeg, freshly ground
3/4 cup of Parmesan cheese, grated
8 cups water and 1/2 tablespoon salt for cooking pasta

1. Place your serving dish filled halfway with hot water in a warm oven.
2. Melt butter in a sauté pan.
3. Add the cream and cook until very hot, almost to a boil. Add pepper and nutmeg. Turn off heat.
4. Fill stock pot with 8 cups cold water. Add 1/2 tablespoon of salt. Place lid on stock pot and bring water to a boil.
5. Add pasta and stir to avoid clumps. Turn down heat and let pasta slowly boil 1-2 minutes.
6. Remove your serving dish from the oven and pour out the hot water.
7. When pasta is al dente (just cooked) lift cooked pasta out of the pot with tongs and place in your serving bowl. It's okay to have some of the pasta water in your dish as well.
8. Reheat the sauce to a simmer and pour hot cream sauce over the pasta. Toss with tongs to coat with sauce. Add Parmesan cheese and gently toss, with tongs. Adjust seasonings and serve.

Lemon Basil Pasta

I have lemons growing year-round thanks to a helpful citrus farmer's advice. She lets her lemons sit on the trees for up to two years only picking what she needs. Juicy lemons combined with the bright flavor of basil make this a favorite dish during summer months.

SERVES 4

Ingredients

1/2 pound pasta, dried
Juice of 1 lemon and zest of 2 lemons
2 tablespoons butter, cut into small pieces
1 tablespoon extra-virgin olive oil
1/2 cup fresh basil leaves, packed and cut into thin strips
1/2 teaspoon salt
1/8 teaspoon pepper
1/2 cup Parmesan cheese, grated

1. Fill stock pot with 8 cups cold water and add 1/2 tablespoon of salt.
2. Place a lid on stock pot and bring water to a boil. Add pasta and stir to avoid clumps.
3. Bring the water back to a boil and then turn down the heat so that it is slowly boiling.
4. Let pasta slowly boil for 8-12 minutes or until tender.
5. While pasta is cooking, take a medium-sized bowl and add lemon zest, juice, butter, olive oil, and basil.
6. When pasta is al dente (just done), remove from stock pot with tongs and place in bowl of ingredients. Some of the pasta water dripping off of the noodles helps give the dish more flavor.
7. Sprinkle in Parmesan cheese and serve.

Quinoa

This high protein grain, popular with the Incas, makes a beautiful warm or cold salad. You must be sure and rinse the quinoa before cooking it or it will taste soapy.

SERVES 4-6

Ingredients

4 cups water
1 cup quinoa
1/2 teaspoon salt

Savory Quinoa Salad

You can make a warm or cold salad by adding these tasty ingredients to your cooked quinoa:

4 tablespoons capers
2 tablespoons chopped parsley or basil
1 1/2 cups marinated artichoke hearts, chopped
1/4 cup extra-virgin olive oil
1/4 teaspoon salt and a bit of fresh ground pepper

1. Place 2 cups of water in a 1 ½- quart saucepan. Add the quinoa and stir to coat each grain with water. Rinse the grains through a fine mesh strainer, then add the grains back to the pot.
2. Add the remaining 2 cups of water and the salt.
3. Place your pot on high heat and bring to a boil, stirring occasionally.
4. Once it has boiled, reduce the heat to low and bring the mixture down to a simmer.
5. Place the lid on saucepan and cook about 15 minutes or until all of the liquid has evaporated.
6. Turn off the heat and let the quinoa sit covered for 5 minutes.
7. Fluff with a fork and transfer into your serving dish.

Corn Bread with Honey Butter

This wheat-free corn bread tastes extra special when it's topped with local honey butter. Bee keeping is very popular in Santa Cruz and my students and I always benefit when there is a beekeeper or two in my classes!

SERVES 6-8

Ingredients

1 ½ cups corn meal

1 teaspoon salt

1 ½ teaspoons baking powder

1 ¾ cups buttermilk

2 eggs

2 tablespoon butter, melted

1. Preheat the oven to 400 degrees. Grease and line a 9-inch cake pan with parchment paper.
2. In a medium-sized bowl sift together the flour, salt, and baking powder.
3. In a separate bowl, stir together the eggs, buttermilk, and melted butter.
4. Make a well in the center of the dry ingredients and pour in the wet ingredients. Whisk to combine.
5. Pour the batter into your prepared pan and bake for 18-21 minutes, or until a toothpick inserted in the center comes out clean.
6. Cool 5 minutes. Run a knife around the edges of the bread and invert onto a platter. Remove the parchment. Slice cornbread into wedges.
7. Serve with honey butter.

Honey Butter

4 ounces soft butter mixed with 2 ounces of honey

Entrees

Entrees

Cheesy Pesto Tart

Cocoa Carne Asada

Teriyaki Salmon

Salmon Sliders with Wasabi Mayonnaise

Chicken Molé

Tomato Basil Galette

Black Bean Chili con Carne

Sushi

Cheesy Pesto Tart

This is a favorite summertime specialty. A pound of any mixture of garden or grocery store tomatoes works well with this recipe.

MAKES ONE 9-INCH TART

Ingredients

Tart Dough

1 1/3 cups of flour
1/4 cup chopped walnuts
1 1/3 sticks butter (5 1/2 ounces) cut into tablespoon size pieces
Extra flour for dusting your hands

Filling

1 pound (4 medium) tomatoes, sliced 1/4 inch thick *
Salt and pepper
1/2 cup pesto (page 3)
3/4 cups ricotta cheese
2 eggs
1/4 cup mozzarella, grated
1/2 cup Parmesan cheese, grated

* If tomatoes are juicy, place the slices in a colander for 10 minutes to drain.

Garnish

3 tablespoons extra-virgin olive
A fresh basil sprig

For Tart Dough

1. Place all ingredients in stand mixer with the paddle attachment. Combine until dough comes together and looks like crumbly cookie dough.
2. Press dough into tart tin with a removable bottom. If the dough is sticky, dip your hands into some flour and continue pressing. Poke holes all over the bottom of the tart with a fork and place in freezer for 15 minutes.
3. Bake tart shell at 375 degrees for 15-20 minutes or until golden brown. You are partially baking the tart so try to not get it too brown.

---

1. Preheat oven to 350 degrees and place a rack at the lowest level in your oven. Mix pesto, ricotta, eggs, mozzarella, and Parmesan cheese in a small bowl.
2. Place half of the tomatoes on partially baked tart shell. Season with salt and pepper.
3. Spread cheese mixture over the tomatoes. Place another layer of tomatoes over the cheese mixture. Season with salt and pepper.
4. Drizzle with olive oil and bake on the lowest rack in your oven to really brown the bottom of the pastry.
5. Bake 40-50 minutes. The tart is done when it is brown along the edges and a knife inserted in the cheesy filling comes out clean.
6. Brush tart with olive oil and garnish with basil sprig.

Cocoa Carne Asada

I developed this recipe when students requested that I add a savory chocolate lesson to my 8-week chocolate course. We like to carve this richly flavored meat into thin slices and fill tortillas, topping them with avocado, Salsa Fresca (page 4), and cabbage. You can also nest the meat in a mound of Creamy Polenta (page 38).

MAKES 4 SERVINGS

Ingredients

1 pound flank steak
2 tablespoons extra-virgin olive oil
Salt and pepper
1 tablespoon cocoa
1 tablespoon chili powder
1/2 teaspoon sugar
1/2 teaspoon cinnamon
1/2 teaspoon salt
1 tablespoon olive oil

1. Place the meat onto a parchment-lined cookie sheet. Cut hatch marks 1/8-inch deep into both sides of the steak. Brush with the 2 tablespoons of olive oil. Season with salt and pepper. Let sit 15 minutes on your counter.
2. Stir together the remaining dry ingredients. Rub seasoning onto both sides of the steak.
3. Heat remaining tablespoon of oil in a 12-inch sauté pan until it shimmers. Cut steak into 4 pieces. Cook steaks, flipping once, until meat registers 145 degrees on a meat thermometer, or about 7-8 minutes, for medium.
4. Let the steak rest on your cutting board, covered loosely with foil for 10 minutes then slice across the grain.

Teriyaki Salmon

Serve this lovely caramelized salmon with coconut rice (page 35).

MAKES 4 SERVINGS

Ingredients

1 pound 8 ounces wild salmon fillets, cut into four, 6 ounce portions

For the Marinade:

1/3 cup soy sauce
2 tablespoons extra-virgin olive oil
2 tablespoons honey
1 teaspoons grated fresh ginger
2 cloves garlic, minced
1/8 teaspoon each salt and pepper

Garnish

1 lemon halved and sliced into rounds

1. Prepare the marinade in a small bowl. Reserve half of the marinade and pour the other half into a 1-gallon zipper-lock bag.
2. Add the salmon to the bag and lay the bag on a cookie sheet. Place in the refrigerator for 30 minutes. Flip the bag over and rest for another 20 minutes on your counter.
3. Adjust your top oven rack one level away from the broiler and turn on the oven heat to broil.
4. When oven is preheated, remove fish from the marinade and place on a foil lined baking sheet.
5. Place fish in the oven and broil for 7-10 minutes or until salmon is no longer raw inside and the internal temperature registers at 125 degrees (medium-rare) with an instant read thermometer.
6. Place the salmon on a decorative platter, brush with reserved marinade, and garnish with lemon slices.

Salmon Sliders with Wasabi Mayonnaise

Here's a recipe to satisfy your craving for salmon without breaking your budget. These are also fun to eat! Count on serving 2 per person for dinner or serve as an appetizer at your next party as mini-burgers.

MAKES 14 MINI BURGERS OR FIVE, 3.5 OUNCE BURGERS

Ingredients

1 pound wild salmon fillet
3/4 cup dry bread crumbs, one slice bread crumbled
2 eggs
1 tablespoons fresh parsley, chopped
1/4 teaspoon garlic granules
1/8 teaspoon salt
Freshly ground pepper
1 cup shredded Cheddar cheese (optional)
4 tablespoons olive oil
14 mini hamburger buns
Various condiments such as: ketchup sliced red onions, Dijon mustard, mayonnaise.

1. Preheat the oven to 175 degrees to warm the oven.
2. Place salmon, bread crumbs, eggs, parsley, garlic, salt, and freshly ground pepper in a large bowl and mix together with one hand until you get an even consistency of all ingredients.
3. Take small handfuls of mixture and flatten into patties about 2 ½ inches in diameter. Set aside on a plate or wax paper.
4. Cook sliders in two batches, depending on the size of your sauté pan.
5. Pour 2 tablespoons of oil in a large sauté pan (approximately 12-inches). Turn the heat on medium high. When oil shimmers place sliders in oil. Cook until sliders are brown on the bottom, about 4 minutes. Flip over sliders and top with cheese, if you are using it. Cover the pan with a lid until cheese melts, about 1 minute.
6. Place cooked sliders on mini hamburger buns and place them in a deep dish pan (13 by 9-inch pan). Cover with foil and place in warm oven.
7. Cook remaining sliders. Place sliders on buns and place in a warm over to heat the entire slider and bun, about 5 minutes. Serve sliders with your favorite condiments. One of ours is wasabi mayonnaise.

Wasabi Mayonnaise

1 teaspoon dried wasabi powder, available at most large grocery stores
1 tablespoon water
3 tablespoons mayonnaise

Mix wasabi powder and water to make a smooth paste. Let sit 5 minutes. Wisk in the mayonnaise.

Chicken Molé

Here is another savory chocolate dish students make in the chocolate class. Students are delighted to learn how to prepare this rich sauce and often have friendly competitions to see who can make the most flavorful molé.

SERVES 10-12

Ingredients

For the Chicken

4 pounds boneless chicken breasts
2 onions, quartered
2 celery stalks, chopped
2 carrots, chopped
4 cloves of garlic, skinned whole
2 bay leaves

For the Molé

5 dried chilies, stemmed, and seeded. A wide variety of dried chilies are available at grocery stores and I'm a fan of these mild ones: pasilla and mulato.
2 tablespoons oil
2 cloves garlic, minced
1 large onion chopped, about 2 cups
3 tablespoons almond butter
2 corn tortillas, toasted and shredded
1 small spring fresh oregano
2 ounces dark chocolate, chopped (a 72% chocolate bar works well)

1. Place all the ingredients in a large stock pot. Top with 12 cups water. Bring to a boil and then simmer about 20 minutes or until chicken is done.
2. Remove cooked chicken and place on large platter, cool, and shred into small pieces.
3. Strain stock and remove 3 cups. Reserve remaining stock for another purpose.
4. Boil the 3 cups of stock about 15 minutes, reducing it to about half.

Molé

1. Place chilies in a shallow bowl, cover with 3 cups of stock, and soak for 15 minutes.
2. Pour the liquid and chilies into a blender.
3. In a large sauté pan, heat oil until it shimmers. Add the garlic and onions and cook over medium high heat until soft.
4. Place onions and garlic in the blender with the chilies. Pulse until smooth.
5. Add almond butter, tortillas, and oregano. Continue to blend.
6. When sauce is smooth, return it to the sauté pan and bring it to a boil. Reduce the heat to barely a simmer. Place a lid on the pan and simmer for 15 minutes. Check every 2-3 minutes and stir.
7. Stir in chunks of chocolate one piece at time, checking the flavor. Season with salt and pepper. Place chicken in the sauce and heat through, about 5 minutes.
8. Serve molé with warm corn tortillas, cilantro, lime wedges, sour cream, and chopped avocado.

Tomato Basil Galette

A galette is a classic French open-faced pie. A student of mine once made this colorful pie and her boyfriend proposed! Their smiles could not be any brighter the day she brought him to class so that I could meet him.

MAKES 1 GALETTE

Ingredients

1 Recipe galette pastry dough (page 85)

For the Filling

1 cup Mozzarella, Monterey Jack, or Cheddar, or a combination, shredded
1/2 cup fresh basil leaves, cut into thin strips
3 plum tomatoes, cut into 1/4 inch slices
2 tablespoons cornmeal
Salt and pepper
Extra-virgin olive oil
Coarse salt or sesame seeds for garnish

Egg-wash

1 egg whisked with 1 tablespoon milk

1. Preheat oven to 400 degrees. Line a half sheet pan with parchment paper.
2. On a lightly floured countertop, roll dough into a 14-inch circle.
3. Pick up the disk and place it on the parchment-lined cookie sheet. Brush with egg wash. Then sprinkle cornmeal in the center of pastry leaving a 2-inch border.
4. In a separate bowl, combine cheeses and basil. Then sprinkle this on the dough, leaving a 2-inch border.
5. Carefully overlap the tomatoes onto the cheese. Sprinkle with salt and pepper, drizzle with olive oil, and fold in the sides of the dough until you have a loose circle with crimped edges.
6. Take remaining egg-wash and brush this on the outside of the galette. Sprinkle with coarse salt or sesame seeds.
7. Bake at 400 degrees for 35-40 minutes.
8. Let rest for 10 minutes before slicing.

Black Bean Chili con Carne

Try making this hearty chili with homemade black beans from the Black Bean Soup recipe, (page 27). The Cornbread (page 44), goes well with the chili for a winter lunch or while watching The Game on TV.

SERVES 10-12

Ingredients

1 tablespoon canola oil
1 large onion, diced
2 cloves garlic, minced
1 pound 8 ounces lean ground turkey meat
Salt and pepper
2 (14.5 ounce) cans chopped tomatoes
2 (15 ounce) cans black beans, drained
8 ounces tomato sauce
1 tablespoon fresh oregano, minced
1 teaspoon ground cumin
2 teaspoons chili powder
2 teaspoons cocoa powder
1/2 teaspoon salt
1/4 teaspoon red pepper flakes

1. In a large stock pot, add the oil and turn the heat to medium high.
2. When the oil is shimmering, add the onions and garlic. Sauté until soft, about 3 minutes.
3. Add the ground turkey and season with salt and pepper. Cook the turkey until there is no more pink meat showing, about 7 minutes.
4. Add remaining ingredients to meat mixture and turn the heat up to high. Bring the chili to a boil.
5. Reduce the heat to a slow simmer and cook uncovered 1 hour.
6. Taste chili and adjust seasonings.
7. Ladle chili into bowls and garnish with, cheese, green onions, and avocados, or let your guests add their own topings.

Garnish

2 cups cheddar cheese or a combination of mild cheeses, shredded
6 green onions, cut into thin slices
2 avocados, peeled and sliced

Sushi

We often have sushi for dinner on the weekends. There are usually a few of us at the house who can chip in to help prepare all of the fresh and tasty ingredients.

MAKES 12-16 ROLLS

Ingredients

Sushi Rice seasoned with sweet vinegar
8 toasted nori sheets cut in half
Fish and vegetables fillings
Bowl of water and vinegar (combine 2/3 cup water with 1/3 cup vinegar)
Tools: Clean wet towel, a bamboo roller wrapped with plastic wrap or an unsealed 1-gallon zipper-lock bag

Sushi Rice

2 cups sushi rice
4 cups water
1 tsp salt

Sushi fillings

You can add any of these fillings to your sushi rolls.

Avocado slices
Toasted sesame seeds
Cucumber spears
Carrot strips
Salmon, cooked and shredded

1. To remove the starch from the rice, rinse it with cold water, in a strainer, until the water is clear.
2. Place rice, water, and salt in a 4-quart saucepan over high heat. Bring to a boil. Turn the heat down so the rice simmers and cover. It takes about 25-30 minutes to cook.
3. About 10 minutes before the rice finishes, when the water has just evaporated, turn off the heat. Remove the lid and place a towel over the pot and cover with the lid. This steams the rice and helps prevent mushy rice.
4. When rice is tender and water has evaporated, pour it into a shallow dish and pour the sweet vinegar over the rice.

Sweet Vinegar

1/3 cup rice wine vinegar
1 teaspoon salt
2 tablespoons sugar

1. In a small pot, mix together all the ingredients and place over a medium flame. You can also microwave the ingredients until the sugar and salt are dissolved. Stir constantly until the salt and sugar are dissolved.
2. Pour this mixture over the hot rice, stirring every 5 minutes or so until the rice stops steaming.
3. Cover with a cloth towel and let sit at room temperature until ready to use.

Preparing Maki (makizushi) Rolls

1. Always have hands slightly damp with a bowl of vinegar water.
2. Lay a bamboo matt on your counter. Place nori sheet flush with bamboo matt. You can cover your bamboo roller in plastic so it does not get gummed up with rice.
3. Spread rice (3/8 inch) on nori, leaving a 1-inch border free from rice at top of nori (away from you).
4. Wet the 1-inch area of nori. Place the fillings in the center. Roll the filled nori away from you. Roll toward you for beginners
5. Roll one full time and then continue rolling and adding pressure. Gently press for 30 seconds to shape it.
6. Firm up the roll by rolling with a bamboo roller
7. Cut in half with sharp wet knife with the seam side down
8. Lay strips side-by-side and cut again, cleaning your knife with a damp towel after each slice is made. Each slice is about 3/4-inch.

Preparing Uramaki Rolls

Uramaki is the inside out roll, created after the California roll was invented to hide the nori.

1. Lay a bamboo matt on your counter. Place a sheet of nori on the matt. Spread rice all over nori (3/8 inch) use side of left hand to firm up the edge while your right hand pats down rice.
2. Sprinkle sesame seeds over rice. Flip nori over, so the nori is facing up and the rice side is resting on the bamboo roller.
3. Place the filling in the middle and roll up, firming round or square shape with the bamboo roller.
4. Follow steps 7 and 8 for the Maki rolls.

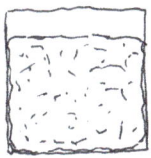  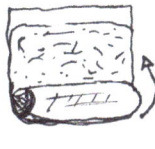 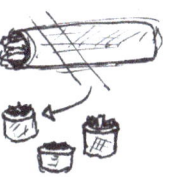

Desserts

Desserts

Plum Crisp

Matt's Apple Crisp

Strawberry Rhubarb Cobbler

Apple Pocket Pies

Dana's Blueberry Buckle

Plum Crisp

Create a plum crisp rainbow by using different colored varieties of plums from your farmers market. This summery dessert feeds a crowd! Teens in my summer cooking camps take a warm plum crisp home to share with their families on the last day of camp.

SERVES 12

Ingredients

2 ½ pounds plums, cut into eighths
2 tablespoons lemon juice
2 tablespoons all-purpose flour
1/2 cup granulated sugar

Streusel Topping

8 ounces butter, cold and cut into tablespoon-sized pieces
2 cups all-purpose flour
1 cup coconut sugar, or granulated sugar
3/4 teaspoon cinnamon
1/2 cup oats

1. Preheat the oven to 375 degrees.
2. In a large bowl mix together the flour and sugar. Add the plums and stir to evenly coat the plums with the dry ingredients. Sprinkle over the lemon juice. Scoop plum mixture into a 13 by 9-inch baking dish
3. In a stand mixer with the paddle attachment, food processor with the metal blade attachment, or by hand with two knives, make the streusel topping. Process the butter, flour, sugar, and cinnamon until crumbly. Hand mix in the oats.
4. Pour streusel on top of plum mixture (it's a lot!) and bake for 40-50 minutes, or until fruit is bubbling and topping is crisp and lightly browned.

Variation

Pear Crisp

Substitute peeled and sliced pears for plums.

Matt's Apple Crisp

My husband Matt likes to make this in the fall when our apple trees hang heavy with fruit and we have trouble keeping up with the harvest.

SERVES 12

Ingredients

2 pounds apples (8 medium-sized) peeled, cored, and cut into 12 slices each
1/3 cup sugar
1/4 cup whole wheat flour or all-purpose flour
1 teaspoon cinnamon
1/2 cup apple juice

* **Streusel topping: see Plum Crisp recipe on page 59**

1. Preheat oven to 350 degrees.
2. In a large bowl mix together the sugar, flour, and cinnamon. Add the apples and stir to evenly coat the apples with the dry ingredients.
3. Scoop apple mixture into a 13 by 9-inch baking dish
4. Pour juice into your dish alongside the edges of the apple mixture.
5. Top with streusel and bake for 40-50 minutes, or until fruit is bubbling and topping is crisp and lightly browned.
6. Serve warm with Vanilla Ice Cream (page 95) or Cinnamon Whipped Cream (see page 89).

Strawberry-Rhubarb Cobbler

Cobblers are American fruit desserts sweetened and topped with biscuit batter. Here is a classic combination. We use Ruby Red rhubarb, which grows heartily in Santa Cruz. I got a little starter plant at my garden club one summer. It dies off in the winter and grows back with vigor every spring. Organic strawberries are also a must.

SERVES 12

Ingredients

Filling

2 pints fresh organic strawberries, hulled and quartered
1 ½ pounds rhubarb, trimmed with a vegetable peeler if woody, and cut into 1/4- inch size pieces
1 1/4 cups granulated sugar
2 tablespoons tapioca starch, or corn starch

Topping

1 cup all-purpose flour
1/3 cup cake flour
1/4 cup coconut sugar, or granulated sugar
2 teaspoons baking powder
1/2 teaspoon baking soda
6 tablespoons (3 ounces) butter, cold and cut into tablespoon-sized pieces
1 cup non-fat yogurt, cold

1. Preheat the oven to 375 degrees.
2. In 13 by 9-inch baking dish, toss together the strawberries, rhubarb, sugar, and tapioca starch.
3. In a stand mixer with the paddle attachment, food processor with the metal blade attachment, or by hand with two knives, make the cobbler topping. Sift together flours, sugar, baking powder, and baking soda. Add the butter and mix until crumbly. Hand mix in the yogurt with a spatula or large spoon.
4. Spoon dollops of batter over the fruit mixture.
5. Bake for 30 minutes or until cobbler is golden brown and juices are bubbling.

Apple Pocket Pies

I started making these with my son's fifth grade class many years ago. His teacher, Ms. Orlando, told me that she had access to a large amount of apples. That's all I needed to hear. We repeated the lesson with my daughter's third grade class the next week. This recipe is now part of my fall repertoire. Turns out adults like to make these too!

MAKES 5 POCKET PIES

Ingredients

1 recipe Galette Pastry Dough (page 85)

Apple filling:

2 apples (3/4 pound) Golden Delicious, Mutsu, Gravenstein, or Jonagold
1/4 cup granulated sugar
1/4 teaspoon cinnamon
1/8 teaspoon nutmeg
Zest from one small lemon

Egg-wash

1 egg whisked with 1 tablespoon milk.

Garnish

1 tablespoon turbinado sugar or granulated sugar

1. Set oven temperature to 375 degrees and line a cookie sheet with parchment paper.
2. Peel, core, slice, and rough chop the apples. Place apples in a bowl and sprinkle with sugar, cinnamon, nutmeg, and lemon zest. Toss the apples until evenly coated with sugar, spices, and zest.
3. Remove pastry dough from the refrigerator. Divide into five, 2-ounce portions and roll each portion into 5 ½-inch disks.
4. Brush the pastry with egg wash. Place 1/4 cup of apple mixture onto one side of the pastry.
5. Fold 1/2 the pastry over the apples, lining up the edges. Press edges with fingertips to seal them crimp with a fork.
6. Brush with egg-wash, decoratively cut three slashes through the dough at a slight angle, and sprinkle with turbinado sugar.
7. Bake for 20 minutes. Cool for 5-10 minutes and enjoy!

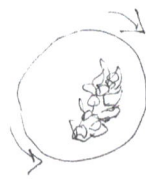

Dana's Blueberry Buckle

My son, Dana, makes this for our 4th of July garden party. We serve it with Vanilla Ice Cream (page 95). It's been known to cool hot tempers after an intense croquet game.

SERVES 12

Ingredients

4 cups (1 ½ pounds) fresh blueberries
1/2 cup granulated sugar
1/2 cup coconut sugar, or brown sugar
1 cup all-purpose flour
1 ½ teaspoons baking powder
1/4 teaspoon salt
4 tablespoons (2 ounces) butter, melted
6 ounces whole milk, room temperature
1/2 teaspoon vanilla

Garnish

1/4 cup of powdered sugar

1. Preheat oven to 375 degrees.
2. Place berries in 13 by 9-inch baking dish and sprinkle with 1/2 cup granulated sugar.
3. In a separate bowl, sift together, the coconut sugar, flour, baking powder, and salt.
4. Melt butter in a small pot, add the milk, and vanilla. Stir to cool to room temperature.
5. Make a well in the center of the dry ingredients and pour in the wet mixture. Stir with a spatula until just smooth. A few lumps are okay.
6. Drizzle the batter over the berries. The batter will not cover the berries completely. Bake for 35 minutes or until batter puffs up and browns.
7. Sift powdered sugar over the top of the buckle and serve warm with vanilla ice cream.

Cookies

Meyer Lemon Refrigerator Cookies

Cacao Nib Butter Cookies

Peanut Butter Gems

Oatmeal Cookies

Cantuccini

Bountiful Jam Squares

Gluten-Free Bountiful Jam Squares

Gluten-Free Flour Blend

Meyer Lemon Refrigerator Cookies

Little lemon rounds of goodness sparkling with crunchy sugar are the perfect accompaniment with your afternoon cup of tea or coffee.

MAKES 80 COOKIES

Ingredients

8 ounces butter, softened
3/4 cup granulated sugar
1 egg
1 lemon juiced (2 tablespoons) and zest from lemon
2 ½ cups plus all-purpose flour

Garnish

1/4 cup turbinado sugar or granulated sugar

1. Using a stand mixer with the paddle attachment, beat the butter and sugar on medium high until the mixture is light and fluffy, about 5 minutes.
2. In a separate bowl combine egg, lemon juice, and zest.
3. Pour into butter mixture and beat until smooth, about 1 minute. Scrape down the sides and beat again 1 minute.
4. Sift flour onto parchment paper.
5. In 3 installments add the flour to the butter/lemon mixture. Stop the mixer each time when adding the flour. Mix just to combine. Be careful not to over mix, or your cookies will have a tough rather than delicate texture.
6. Remove dough from the bowl and divide in half, about 14 ounces each. Roll each piece into a 10 by 1 ½-inch log using parchment to help guide you and keep the dough in a log shape. Unwrap log from parchment paper and sprinkle sugar all over the paper. Roll up the log in the sugared paper so that some sugar coats the outside of the cookie dough log.
7. Wrap the cookie dough in parchment paper. Place in the refrigerator for at least 1 hour.
8. Slice cookies into 1/4-inch slices bake at 350 for 12-15 minutes or until tops are barely golden and bottoms of cookies are lightly browned.

Cacao Nib Butter Cookies

Cacao nibs are broken pieces of the raw cacao bean from which chocolate is made. Toast the nibs like nuts to bring out their flavor. My culinary students give these cookies as thank you gifts when we go on our class field trips.

MAKES 80 COOKIES

Ingredients

8 ounce butter, softened
3/4 cup granulated sugar
1 egg
1 teaspoon vanilla extract
2½ cups all-purpose flour
2 ounces bittersweet chocolate, finely chopped
2 ounces cacao nibs, toasted in a 350 degree oven on a cookie sheet for 5-10 minutes
1/2 teaspoon espresso powder

Garnish

1/4 cup turbinado sugar or granulated sugar

1. Using a stand mixer, with the paddle attachment, mix butter and sugar on medium-high until the mixture is light and fluffy, about 5 minutes.
2. In a separate bowl combine egg and vanilla.
3. Pour into butter mixture and beat until smooth, about 1 minute. Scrape down the sides and beat again 1 minute.
4. Sift flour onto parchment paper and mix chocolate, nibs, and espresso powder into flour.
5. In 3 installments add the flour/chocolate mixture to the butter mixture. Stopping the mixer each time when adding the flour. Mix just until the dough comes together. Be careful not to over mix or your cookies will have a tough rather than delicate texture.
6. Remove dough from the bowl and divide in half, about 14 ounces each. Roll each piece into an 11-by-1 ½ -by -1-inch rectangle using parchment and a ruler to help guide you and keep the dough in a rectangle shape. Unwrap dough from parchment paper and sprinkle sugar all over the paper. Roll the dough into a log shape in the sugared paper so that some sugar adheres to all of the cookie dough.
7. Wrap up the cookie dough in parchment paper. Place in the refrigerator for at least 1 hour.
8. Slice cookies into 1/4-inch slices bake at 350 bake 12-15 minutes or until tops are barely golden and bottoms of cookies are golden brown.

Peanut Butter Gems

I brought these cookies to my neighbor Emily's Girl Scout gathering when her mom Lee Ann asked me to speak about careers in culinary arts. I chose these cookies because many children are eating gluten-free. Their endearing thank you notes gave me a hint that I chose the right recipe to share.

MAKES 15 COOKIES

Ingredients

1 cup salted creamy peanut butter
1 cup coconut sugar, sifted if lumpy, or granulated sugar
1 large egg
1/2 teaspoon vanilla

Garnish

2 tablespoons coconut sugar or granulated sugar

1. Preheat oven to 350 degrees and line a cookie sheet with parchment paper. Set aside.
2. In a medium-sized bowl stir together the peanut butter and one cup of coconut sugar. If your sugar has a few lumps, just smash them with the back of your spoon or spatula while stirring.
3. Stir in the egg and vanilla. Once the mixture is combined, let it rest for 5 minutes.
4. Scoop a heaping tablespoon of dough into the palm of your hand and roll it into a ball. Roll the balls into the 2 tablespoons of coconut sugar to coat them. Use more sugar if necessary. Place the balls of dough on your baking sheet.
5. Once you have shaped the cookies you are ready to add the classic American peanut butter cookie cross hatching on top of each cookie.
6. Press the tins of a fork into each ball of cookie dough. Dip fork in water if sticky. Repeat pressing the fork in the opposite direction.
7. Bake for 5 minutes on the middle rack of your oven. Rotate the cookie sheet and bake for another 5 minutes. The cookies should be crisp on the outside and moist in the center.

Oatmeal Cookies

Here's a classic cookie filled with wholesome goodness. They are very soft and not too sweet, which makes them perfect for breakfast!

MAKES ABOUT 46 COOKIES

Ingredients

4 ounces (1 stick) butter, melted

1 cup coconut sugar or granulated sugar

1/2 cup olive oil, canola, or sunflower oil

3 large eggs

2 teaspoons vanilla

2 cups all-purpose flour

1 teaspoon baking soda

1 teaspoon baking powder

3 cups oats

1 ¼ cups raisins

1 cup chopped walnuts

1. Preheat oven to 350 degrees. Line 4 cookie sheets with parchment paper and set aside.
2. In a medium-sized bowl whisk together butter, sugar, oil, eggs, and vanilla.
3. In a separate bowl sift together flour, baking soda, and baking powder.
4. Add flour mixture, in 3 additions, to the egg mixture. Mixing until combined.
5. When dry ingredients are mixed in, add the oats and raisins. Stir until fully incorporated.
6. Scoop heaping tablespoon-sized drops of dough and place on cookie sheets.
7. Adjust oven racks so that you can bake 2 cookie sheets at a time. I have one rack on the second level and one on the fourth level. Bake cookies for 5 minutes rotate the pans from top to bottom racks and bake another 5 minutes.
8. Let cookies rest on pan for 5 minutes, then remove them onto a rack to cool.

I like to under-bake these cookies until they are barely brown on top; it keeps them moist and chewy. Keep at room temperature for 4 days in a tightly closed container. Freeze cookies that you will not eat within a day and take them out of the freezer as needed.

Ingredients

2 cups all-purpose flour
1 cup sugar
1 teaspoon baking powder
1 teaspoon cinnamon
1/4 teaspoon salt
1 ½ cups whole almonds
3 large eggs
Zest of one lemon
1 ½ teaspoons almond extract

Gluten Free Flour Blend

4 ½ cups white rice flour
2 cups brown rice flour
1 ½ cups potato starch
1 ½ cups tapioca flour, also called tapioca starch
3 tablespoons nonfat milk powder
1 ½ teaspoons xanthan gum

1. Sift all ingredients into a large bowl.
2. Then sift another two times to make sure all ingredients are mixed together.
3. Keeps 6 months in a tightly sealed container.

Cantuccini

These classic Tuscan biscotti are great to wrap in decorative bags and give as gifts.

MAKES 36 COOKIES

1. Preheat oven to 350 degrees. Line a cookie sheet with parchment paper.
2. Sift together the flour, sugar, baking powder, cinnamon, and salt. Add the almonds.
3. In a separate bowl whisk together the eggs, lemon zest, and almond extract.
4. Make a well in the center of the dry ingredients and stir in the egg mixture with a large spatula. The dough will be dry. Once you have it somewhat moistened, place your hand in the bowl and knead the dough until it forms a ball. Place the ball onto your parchment and pat into a square. Cut the square in half and shape each piece into a 12 by 2-inch log with your hands pressing and picking up the dough as needed.
5. Bake the logs for 30 minutes.
6. Remove logs from oven. Let cool for 5 minutes then move onto a cooling rack.
7. Cool about 30 minutes and cut into ½-inch diagonal slices.
8. Place slices back on baking sheet and bake another 10 minutes on one side, then flip the cookies over and bake another 10 minutes.

Bountiful Jam Squares

When you are short on time and need a bounty of cookies these are the ones to pop in the oven.

MAKES ABOUT 24 JAM SQUARES

Ingredients

4 ounces (1 stick) butter, softened
2 cups sugar
2 teaspoons vanilla
2 eggs, room temperature
4 tablespoons milk, room temperature
3 cups all-purpose flour
1 cup whole wheat flour
2 teaspoons baking powder
1 ½ cups low sugar jam
Flour for dusting your hands
1/4 cup powdered sugar, for sprinkling over cookies

1. Preheat oven to 375 degrees. Spray an 18 by 13-inch cookie sheet with pan spray and lay down a piece of parchment paper. Spray parchment with pan spray. Set aside.
2. Using a stand mixer with the paddle attachment, cream the butter, sugar, and vanilla until light and fluffy.
3. Combine the eggs and milk in a separate bowl. With the mixer running on low speed, slowly add the egg/milk mixture to the butter mixture. Continue mixing until all ingredients are mixed combined and smooth.
4. Sift the flour and baking powder together over a piece of parchment.
5. With the mixer running on low speed, carefully lift the parchment and pour in the dry ingredients. Stop mixer when dough is crumbly.
6. Scrape out 3/4 of the dough onto your parchment-lined cookie sheet.
7. With floured fingertips, or a greased spatula, spread dough to within 1/2 an inch of the edges of your pan, being careful not to make the center too thick.
8. Spread jam onto the dough. Sprinkle clumps of remaining dough over the jam. Bake cookies for 20 minutes. Rotate cookie sheet and bake another 10-15 minutes. The edges and top will be golden.
9. Cool 30 minutes. Top with powdered sugar. Cut into twenty four, 3 by 3-inch squares

Gluten-Free Bountiful Jam Squares

Here is a sweet variation for our gluten-free friends!

MAKES ABOUT 24 JAM SQUARES

Ingredients

4 ounces (1 stick) butter, softened
2 cups sugar
2 teaspoons vanilla
2 eggs, room temperature
2 tablespoons milk, room temperature
3 cups gluten-free flour (page 71)
2 teaspoons baking powder
1 ½ cups low sugar jam
Flour for dusting your hands
1/4 cup powdered sugar, for sprinkling over cookies

1. Preheat oven to 375 degrees. Spray an 18 by 13-inch cookie sheet with pan spray and lay down a piece of parchment paper. Spray parchment with pan spray. Set aside.
2. Using a stand mixer with the paddle attachment, cream the butter, sugar, and vanilla until light and fluffy.
3. Combine the eggs and milk in a separate bowl. With the mixer running on low speed, slowly add the egg/milk mixture to the butter mixture. Continue mixing until all ingredients are mixed together and smooth.
4. Sift the flour and baking powder together over a piece of parchment.
5. With the mixer running on low speed, carefully lift the parchment and pour in the dry ingredients. Stop mixer when dough is wet. Let sit 10 minutes. This helps the gluten free grains to soften.
6. Scrape out 3/4 of the dough onto your parchment lined cookie sheet.
7. With floured fingertips, or a greased spatula, spread dough to within 1/2 an inch of the edges of your pan, being careful not to make the center too thick.
8. Spread jam onto the dough. Sprinkle remaining dough over the jam. Bake cookies for 20 minutes. Rotate cookie sheet and bake another 15-20 minutes. The edges and top will be golden.
9. Cool 30 minutes. Top with powdered sugar. Cut into twenty-four, 3 by-3 inch squares.

Cakes

Cakes

Apple Spice Cake with Cream Cheese Icing

Simple Plum Cake

Glamorous French Chocolate Cake

Jeanne's Strawberry Shortcake

Apple Spice Cake with Cream Cheese Icing

Here is a cake for a crowd! It's full of chunky apples, healthy nuts, and slathered with cream cheese icing, perfect for your next fall potluck!

SERVES 12-15

Ingredients

1 ½ cups canola or olive oil
2 cups sugar
3 large eggs
1/4 cup apple juice
2 cups all-purpose flour
1 cup whole wheat flour
1 teaspoon cinnamon
1/8 teaspoon allspice
1/8 teaspoon nutmeg
1 teaspoon baking soda
1/2 teaspoon salt
1 cup chopped walnuts
3 cups chopped apples

1. Preheat oven to 325 degrees. Spray a 13 by 9-inch baking dish with pan spray and set aside.
2. In a large bowl whisk together the oil, sugar, eggs, and juice.
3. Sift, over parchment paper, the all-purpose flour, whole wheat flour, cinnamon, allspice, nutmeg, baking soda, and salt.
4. Add dry ingredients to wet. The batter will be very thick. Stir with a spatula.
5. Stir in the apples and nuts. Pour batter into prepared pan and bake 50-60 minutes or until a toothpick inserted into the center comes out clean. Cool for 1 hour. Spread with cream cheese icing.

Cream Cheese Icing

8 ounces cream cheese, softened
4 ounces (1 stick) unsalted butter, softened
1 cup powdered sugar, sifted
1/2 teaspoon vanilla

1. Using a stand mixer with the paddle attachment, mix the cream cheese and butter together until light and fluffy, about 5 minutes. Add the sugar and vanilla and mix until combined. Spread onto cooled cake with a spatula.

Simple Plum Cake

When we need a quick or spontaneous dessert, this is an easy cake to whip up. You can use just about any fruit sprinkled on top of the batter or placed artfully in concentric circles. Let your creativity shine!

SERVES 6-8

Ingredients

3/4 cup (3 ½ ounces) all-purpose flour
1/4 cup (1 ¼ ounces) whole wheat flour
1/2 teaspoon baking powder
1/4 teaspoon baking soda
4 tablespoons butter, (1/2 stick) softened
3/4 cup (4 ounces) coconut sugar, or granulated sugar
1 egg, room temperature
1/2 cup buttermilk, room temperature
6 small Santa Rosa plums, sliced thinly

Garnish

2 tablespoons turbinado sugar or granulated sugar

1. Preheat oven to 375 degrees.
2. Spray a 9-inch pie plate with pan spray.
3. Sift together the flours, baking powder, and baking soda. Set aside.
4. In a medium-sized bowl, cream together the butter and sugar, with a plastic spatula, until the sugar is moist and light in color.
5. Stir in the egg and buttermilk.
6. Stir in the dry ingredients just until moistened and pour batter into prepared pan.
7. Scatter plums on top of batter and sprinkle with turbinado sugar.
8. Bake cake 25-30 minutes. Cake is done when it puffs up, is golden brown and a toothpick inserted in the center comes out clean.

Variation

You can substitute 6 sliced apricots or 2 sliced apples for the plums.

Glamorous French Chocolate Cake

Here is our go-to cake for special family celebrations. It's a rich flourless cake coated in a creamy chocolate icing the French call ganache which translates to "cushion". This a perfect cake to end a lovely evening event.

SERVES 8

Ingredients

4 ounces semisweet chocolate
4 ounces (1 stick) unsalted butter, room temperature
2/3 cups coconut sugar, or granulated sugar
Zest from 1 orange
1 tablespoon orange juice
1 tablespoon coffee
3 eggs, room temperature
6 ounces (1 ¾ cups) almond meal, also called almond flour

Garnish

1/3 cup sliced and toasted almonds

1. Preheat oven 350 degrees. Spray an 8-inch cake pan with pan spray. Cut an 8-inch circle of parchment paper, set this in your pan and spray again with pan spray.
2. Melt chocolate and butter in a double boiler. Remove from heat and stir in sugar.
3. Add the zest, juice, and coffee. Stir in eggs 1 at a time.
4. Stir in the almond meal and pour into prepared pan.
5. Bake 35-40 minutes. The cake is done when it releases from the sides, there's a slight cracking along the edges and a tooth pick inserted in the center comes out with a few crumbs attached.
6. Let cool for 1 hour then run a knife around the edges and invert onto a cardboard round, trimming the cardboard so that it is the same size as your cake. Glaze with ganache icing.

Ganache Icing

8 ounces semisweet chocolate, finely chopped
8 ounces heavy cream, heated to just below a boil

1. Pour the hot cream over the chocolate. Let sit 1 minute then slowly stir until creamy. Don't stir too fast or you will create bubbles. You want the ganache to be smooth and shiny.
2. Pour ganache over cake when it is the consistency of heavy cream. It's best to start in the center and slowly pour out to the edges. Smooth sides with a spatula. Press nuts around sides. Keep the cake at room temperature until ready to serve.

Jeanne's Strawberry Shortcake

Some desserts evoke special memories and this is one of them. My 10-year-old daughter proudly carried this strawberry shortcake from the kitchen to the garden where her grandparents, aunts, uncles, brother, and cousins eagerly awaited a generous slice.

SERVES 10

Ingredients

Strawberry Filling

3 pints organic strawberries, hulled and sliced
1/4 cup sugar

Cake

2 cups all-purpose flour
1/4 cup coconut sugar, or granulated sugar
2 teaspoons baking powder
1/4 teaspoon baking soda
6 tablespoons butter, cold and cut into tablespoon size pieces
2/3 cup buttermilk
1/2 teaspoon vanilla

Garnish

2 tablespoons heavy cream
2 tablespoons turbinado sugar or granulated sugar

1. Preheat oven to 400 degrees. Line a cookie sheet with parchment paper and set aside.
2. In a large bowl, mix together the dry ingredients: flour, sugar, baking powder, and baking soda.
3. Rub the butter into the dry ingredients with your hands until mixture has the texture of marbles, peas, and cornmeal.
4. In another small bowl, mix the buttermilk, and vanilla. Make a well in the center of the dry ingredients. Pour in the wet ingredients. Mix with a spatula until ingredients are just moistened.
5. With a large spatula, scoop out the dough out onto your prepared cookie sheet. Gently press the dough with floured hands or spatula into an 8-inch circle. Try not to handle the dough too much.
6. Brush circle of dough with cream and sprinkle with coarse sugar.
7. Bake at 400 degrees for 15-20 minutes. The cake should puff up and be golden brown.
8. Let the cake cool on the pan for 10 minutes, then carefully place on your serving platter

Cream Filling

1 ½ cups heavy cream
1 ½ tablespoons sugar
1 teaspoon vanilla

Place cream, sugar, and vanilla in a bowl and whip, with a whisk or mixer, until stiff.

Assembling the Cake

When cake cools, carefully slice in half with a long bread knife. Pour juice from marinating strawberries on the bottom half of the cake and then arrange strawberries on top. Spread on 3/4 of the whipped cream. Put top of cake on top of cream. Slice cake in wedges and top with a dollop of remaining whipped cream.

Galettes and Tarts

Galettes & Tarts

Galette Pastry Dough

Very Berry Galette

Streusel Topping

Fruit Galette Variations: Blackberry, Pear, Apple, Nectarine, Plum, Apricot

Tart Dough

Pumpkin Chiffon Tart

Southern Pecan Tart with Cinnamon Whipped Cream

Chocolate Walnut Tart

Fresh Fruit Tart

Galette Pastry Dough

This buttery pastry rolls out beautifully when making galettes, pies, and turnovers. I use all butter in my pastry dough for the fabulous flavor and texture it provides. Experiment with European-style butter, which contains more butterfat than American-style, for a flakier texture.

MAKES ONE 12-INCH ROUND GALETTE

Ingredients

1 1/4 cups (5.5 ounces) all-purpose flour
1/4 teaspoon salt
1 stick (4 ounces) butter, cold, cut into tablespoon-size pieces
1/4 cup ice water

Food Processor Method:

1. Process dry ingredients in a food processor until combined, about 5 seconds.
2. Add butter and process until mixture resembles a combinations of marbles, peas, and cornmeal.
3. Pour water through feed tube until dough holds together, but is not sticky.
4. Lay a 12 by 12-inch piece of plastic wrap on your counter and scrape the dough onto it. Shape into a 1/2-inch thick round disk. Wrap with the plastic wrap.
5. Refrigerate dough 30 minutes to one hour.

Stand Mixer Method:

1. Using a stand mixer with the paddle attachment mix dry ingredients on low speed 5 seconds.
2. Add butter and mix on low speed until mixture resembles a combination of marbles peas, and cornmeal.
3. Add water with mixer on speed low and mix until dough holds together, but is not sticky.
4. Lay a 12 by 12-inch piece of plastic wrap on your counter and scrape the dough onto it. Shape into a ½-inch thick round disk. Wrap with the plastic wrap.
5. Refrigerate 30 minutes to one hour.

Very Berry Galette

Summertime is the right time for berry anything! I especially love berry galettes topped with the Vanilla Ice Cream (page 95).

MAKES ONE 12-INCH ROUND GALETTE

Ingredients

1 recipe Galette Pastry Dough (page 85)

Filling

**8 ounces (1 2/3 cups) blueberries
8 ounces (2 cups) raspberries
1/2 cup sugar
1 tablespoon cornstarch
1 tablespoon tapioca (quick tapioca)
1 tablespoon cornmeal**

Egg-wash

1 egg whisked with 1 tablespoon milk

Garnish

**1 tablespoon turbinado sugar or granulated sugar
1 recipe streusel topping**

Streusel Topping

**2 ounces butter (1/2 stick) cold, cut into tablespoon sized pieces
2 tablespoons sugar
2 tablespoons brown sugar
1/4 teaspoon cinnamon
1/2 cup all-purpose flour
1/4 cup rolled oats**

Blend all ingredients, except the oats, together, with a food processor, stand mixer with the paddle attachment, or by hand, until the butter is thoroughly blended in and the mixture is crumbly. Hand mix in the oats.

1. Preheat oven to 400 degrees. Wash and dry fruit.
2. In a medium-sized bowl combine sugar, cornstarch, and tapioca. Add berries and toss to coat with sugar mixture.
3. Roll out dough into a 14-inch circle on a lightly floured counter top.
4. Place disk on parchment lined cookie sheet. Brush disk with egg wash. Sprinkle cornmeal in center of pastry leaving a 2-inch border.
7. Sprinkle berry mixture onto the center of the dough, leaving a 2-inch border.
8. Fold in the sides of the dough until you have a loose circle with crimped edges.
9. Use remaining egg-wash to brush on the outside of the galette. Sprinkle the sides of pastry with turbinado sugar.
10. Sprinkle the fruit center with streusel topping.
11. Bake at 400 degrees for 35-40 minutes. Let rest for 10 minutes before slicing.

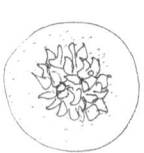  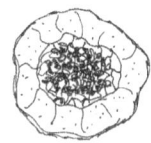

Galette Variations

Replace step #2 with these various fruit fillings.
Some of the fruits do not need thickening agents due to their high natural pectin content.

Blackberry

Toss one pound blackberries with 3/4 cup sugar, omitting the cornstarch and tapioca.

Pear

Toss 3 pears (1 ½ pounds) that have been thinly sliced with 1/3 cup sugar, omitting the cornstarch and tapioca.

Apple

Toss 4 to 5 apples (1 pound) peeled, cored, and thinly sliced with 1/2 cup sugar. Omit the cornstarch and tapioca. I use Golden Delicious harvested from my tree. Often times they are too ripe in the market, so I recommend using a couple different varieties, if you do not have an apple tree where you can choose the exact ripeness of the fruit. Experiment! Tasting apples at your farmers markets and chatting with the farmers is an excellent way to learn about apple varieties.

Nectarine

Toss 2 pounds nectarines with 1/3 cup sugar, 1/2 tablespoon quick tapioca, and 1/2 tablespoon cornstarch.

Plum

Toss 1 pound plums, pitted and quartered with 3/4 cup sugar, and 1 tablespoon cornstarch. Omit tapioca.

Apricot

Toss 1 pound apricots pitted and quartered with 2/3 cup sugar, omitting the cornstarch and tapioca.

Pumpkin Chiffon Tart

Try this elegant and very American pumpkin tart for your Thanksgiving gathering. After all, Americans invented the "Chiffon" pie in the early 1900's and we are thankful! This dessert is light in texture, delicate in flavor, and beautiful to admire.

MAKES ONE 9-INCH TART

Ingredients

A fully-baked 9-inch tart shell. See page 90. Cream cheese filling Pumpkin filling Whipped cream topping

Cream Cheese Filling

6 ounces cream cheese, room temperature
1/3 cup powdered sugar, sifted
1/4 teaspoon vanilla

1. Using a stand mixer, with the paddle attachment, mix cream cheese until light and fluffy.
2. Add sifted powdered sugar, and vanilla. Set aside.

Pumpkin Mousse Filling

1 tablespoon unflavored gelatin
2 tablespoons cold water
2 eggs
6 tablespoons sugar
3/4 cup canned pumpkin
1 tablespoon milk
1/2 teaspoon cinnamon
Pinch of freshly ground nutmeg

1. In a small bowl dissolve gelatin in 2 tablespoons cold water. Set aside.
2. Separate eggs. Place whites in bowl of a stand mixer.
3. Place yolks in a saucepan with the pumpkin, 3 tablespoons sugar, milk, cinnamon, and nutmeg. Gently heat for 5 minutes, evaporating some of the liquid.
4. Remove pumpkin filling from the heat and add the dissolved gelatin, stirring occasionally. Cool to room temperature.
5. In your stand mixer, with the whip attachment, whip the whites, until frothy. Slowly add the 3 tablespoons sugar with the machine running. You are making a meringue. Whip until stiff peaks form.
6. Fold meringue into cooled pumpkin filling with a large spatula.

Whipped Cream: The Layer of Goodness

1/2 cup heavy cream, cold
1/2 tablespoon sugar
1/2 teaspoon vanilla

In your stand mixer, with the whip attachment, whip cream, sugar, and vanilla together until stiff peaks form. Place cream in a piping bag with the star tip.

Assemble the Tart: One, Two, Three

1. Spread the cream cheese filling on the base of prebaked tart shell.
2. Spread pumpkin mousse onto the cream cheese layer.
3. Top with whipped cream in dollops or pipe rosettes around the base. Whew! You have made a masterpiece!

Southern Pecan Tart with Cinnamon Whipped Cream

A buttery crust filled with a rich gooey filling and topped with glistening pecans is a must on the dessert sideboard at Thanksgiving. A student recently commented in a class survey that cinnamon whipped cream was the best invention ever!

MAKES ONE 9-INCH ROUND TART

Ingredients

Partially-baked 9-inch tart shell (page 90).

Filling

2 eggs, room temperature
1/2 cup dark corn syrup
1/4 cup light corn syrup
1/2 cup light brown sugar
2 tablespoons butter, melted
1 tablespoon bourbon, or coffee
1 teaspoon vanilla
1 ¼ cups pecans

Cinnamon Whipped Cream

1 cup heavy cream, cold
1 tablespoon sugar
1 teaspoon vanilla
1/4 teaspoon cinnamon

Place all ingredients in your mixing bowl and whip until soft peaks form.

1. In a medium-sized bowl, whisk together eggs, corn syrups, sugar, butter, bourbon (or coffee), and vanilla.
2. Pour the mixture into a partially-baked tart shell and sprinkle with pecans (you may not need all the pecans) and bake at 350 degrees for 20 minutes or until filling is firm.
3. Cool 20 minutes before removing tart from the pan.
4. Serve with a dollop of cinnamon whipped cream.

Chocolate Walnut Tart

This tart is a bit like a candy bar, full of rich ingredients. Lightly drizzled chocolate scattered across the surface is striking and fun to apply!

MAKES ONE 9-INCH ROUND TART

Ingredients

Partially-baked 9-inch tart shell.

Filling

2 eggs
1/4 cup heavy cream
3/4 cups sugar
1 teaspoon vanilla
2 cups walnuts
1/2 cup (3 ounces) semi-sweet chocolate or chocolate chips, melted

1. Spread 3/4 of melted chocolate on bottom of partially-baked tart shell and set aside. Use remainder of the chocolate to decorate the finished tart.
2. In a medium-sized bowl, whisk together eggs, cream, sugar and vanilla. Add walnuts.
3. Pour mixture into tart shell and bake at 350 degrees for 20-25 minutes or until tart puffs up and browns evenly.
4. Cool. Drizzle remaining melted chocolate over tart with a fork. Remove the tart from the tin and serve.

Tart Dough - MAKES ONE 9-INCH TART

1 1/3 cups all-purpose flour
1/4 cup powdered sugar
1 1/3 sticks butter (5 ½ ounces) cold, cut into tablespoon-size pieces

1. Using a stand mixer with the paddle attachment combine ingredients until dough comes together and looks like crumbly cookie dough. You can also process the ingredients in a food processor.
2. Press the dough evenly into a 9-inch-tart pan with a removable bottom. If the dough is sticky, dust your hands with flour and continue on. Poke holes all over the bottom of the tart with a fork. Place tart in freezer for 15 minutes.
3. Preheat oven 375 degrees.
4. For a partially-baked tart shell that you will fill and bake again, bake tart shell for 15-20 minutes or until lightly browned. For a fully-baked tart shell, that you will not bake again, make sure the tart is a deep golden brown color, cooking it for 25-35 minutes.

Fresh Fruit Tart

This is a favorite dessert at summertime parties when we have such an abundance of colorful and tasty fruits. It was also a favorite dessert of mine that I learned how to make in pastry school. After graduation I was so enamored by the pretty fluted edged French tarts that I started a wholesale bakery called The Queen of Tarts! Coffee houses, caterers, restaurants, and hotels soon called with orders for this eye-catching dessert.

MAKES ONE 9-INCH ROUND TART

Ingredients

One fully baked 9-inch tart shell (page 90.)
Creamy Filling
8 ounces cream cheese
1/2 cup powdered sugar
1/2 teaspoon vanilla
1 tablespoon lemon juice

Glaze

1/4 cup apricot jam
2 tablespoons water

In a small pot, heat apricot jam with water. When it boils, immediately strain into a small container and brush glaze onto fruit. Enjoy!

1. Using a stand mixer, with the paddle attachment, mix cream cheese until light and fluffy.

Add sifted powdered sugar, vanilla, and lemon juice. Mix until just smooth. Do not over mix because the filling may separate.

Spread filling onto tart shell, about ¼-inch thick.

Fresh Fruit

Decorate tart with 3 cups of fresh seasonal fruits.

Ice Cream, Sorbet & Sauces

Vanilla Ice Cream

Mexican Chocolate Ice Cream

Fresh Strawberry Sorbet

Chocolate Sauce

Caramel Sauce

Ice Cream Cones, Cups, and Fortune Cookies

Vanilla Ice Cream

Here is a super quick method for making ice cream Philadelphia-style, an ice cream made without eggs. The texture is a bit softer and the flavor is lighter tasting than the French-style. If you have your canister in the freezer and a pint of cream and some milk in the refrigerator, you can whip this up in 30 minutes, which in my house, brings about great joy!

MAKES 1 QUART

Ingredients

2 cups heavy cream, cold
1 cup whole milk, cold
3/4 cup sugar
1 teaspoon vanilla bean paste *

1. Place all ingredients in a bowl and whisk until the sugar is dissolved, about 2 minutes.
2. Place mixture into the canister of your ice cream maker and follow manufacturer's directions. It usually takes 12-20 minutes to freeze, depending on how cold your mixture is when you pour it into the machine.

* Vanilla bean paste is available in gourmet shops and health food stores. Substitute 1 teaspoon vanilla extract if you do not have any on hand.

Mexican Chocolate Ice Cream

Lovely Latin American flavors surprise the taste buds with this easy ice cream.

MAKES 1 QUART

Ingredients

1/2 cup cocoa
1/2 cup sugar
1 teaspoon cinnamon
2 pinches cayenne powder
Pinch salt
2 cups heavy cream, cold
1 cup whole milk, cold
1 teaspoon vanilla
1 cup slivered almonds, toasted

1. Sift the cocoa, sugar, cinnamon, cayenne powder, and salt into a medium-sized bowl.
2. Slowly whisk in the cream.
3. When ingredients are thoroughly blended add milk and vanilla.
4. Whisk to combine then pour mixture into the canister of your ice cream maker and follow manufacturer's directions for freezing. It usually takes 12-20 minutes to freeze, depending on how cold your mixture is when you pour it into the machine.
5. When the ice cream is churned to your liking, remove the canister from the base and stir in the nuts with a large spoon or spatula.
6. Eat the ice cream soft-serve style or place in your freezer for a couple hours to firm up.

Fresh Strawberry Sorbet

We have some amazing organic strawberry famers in Santa Cruz County and it's a joy to use their delicious berries in this colorful sorbet.

MAKES 1 QUART

Ingredients

2 pounds strawberries, hulled
2 cups simple syrup, cold, see recipe below
2 tablespoons lemon juice

1. Place all ingredients in your blender and blend until smooth.
2. Pour mixture into a shallow bowl and place in your refrigerator for 1 hour.
3. After chilling, pour mixture into your ice cream maker and follow manufacturer's directions for freezing. It usually takes 12-20 minutes to freeze, depending on how cold your mixture is when you pour it into the machine.

Simple Syrup

4 cups sugar
4 cups water

1. Place the sugar and water in a three-quart saucepan and turn the heat on medium high.
2. Stir until the sugar dissolves then bring mixture to a simmer.
3. Remove pot from the heat and pour syrup into a shallow dish to cool.
4. When cool you can store the yrup in a jar in the refrigerator for 5 days or in the freezer for 6 months.

Chocolate Sauce

Homemade silky soft chocolate sauce drizzled over ice cream is a special treat.

MAKES 1 1/8 CUPS

Ingredients

1/2 cup granulated sugar

1/4 cup (2 ounces) water

1/4 cup (2 ounces) light corn syrup

6 ounces semisweet or milk chocolate, finely chopped

2 tablespoons (1 ounce) unsalted butter, room temperature

1. In a 2-quart saucepan combine the sugar, water, and corn syrup.
2. Stir over high heat until sugar is dissolved. Wash down the sides of your pot with a wet pastry brush to remove any undissolved sugar crystals clinging to the sides. Bring mixture to a boil.
3. Remove pan from heat. Add chocolate and butter. Whisking until smooth.

Caramel Sauce

Just a touch of caramel sauce adds a lovely nutty buttery flavor to desserts. Try this drizzled over vanilla ice cream or brushed on top of the Apple Galette (see page 87).

MAKES 1 1/8 CUPS

Ingredients

1 cup water
1 cup sugar
1 tablespoon corn syrup
1/2 cup (4 ounces) heavy cream, warmed
2 tablespoons (1/4 stick) butter, softened
1/2 teaspoon vanilla extract

1. In a 2-quart saucepan, pour in the water, sugar, and corn syrup.
2. Place saucepan over high heat and swirl until the sugar is dissolved.
3. Brush down the sides of the pot with a wet pastry brush, place the lid on the pot and turn the heat to high.
4. When the syrup boils remove the lid, brush down the sides again and do not stir.
5. When the sugar turns an amber color, about 320 degrees using a candy thermometer, remove from the heat and slowly whisk in the heated cream. The mixture will create a lot of steam.
6. When the cream is incorporated, stir in the butter and finally the vanilla when the butter is dissolved into the sauce.
7. Keep in a tightly closed container in the refrigerator for up to 1 month. Reheat in a microwave or over a double boiler until soft.

Ice Cream Cones, Cups & Fortune Cookies

Ice cream cones are just super joyful! These cones are crispy with a great buttery flavor. Try making all three shapes and see what happens. I bet you will come up with some creative vessels. To shape ice cream cones, look for a waffle cone maker that comes with a cone-rolling form, or use a funnel-shaped tool in your kitchen.

MAKES 14 SMALL

Ingredients

6 tablespoons (3 ounces) butter, softened
1 cup powdered sugar, sifted
Pinch of salt
1/2 teaspoon vanilla
3 egg whites (3 ounces), room temperature
1/2 cup (2 ounces) all-purpose flour

For the Batter

1. In a medium-sized bowl mix the butter to a creamy consistency. Slowly add the sugar and salt.
2. Add egg whites little by little. Mix after each addition then stir in vanilla.
3. Sift the flour over the mixture and stir to combine. It will look like cake batter.
4. Batter may be stored in the refrigerator for 3 days or

Making Ice Cream Cones Using a Waffle Cone Maker & Cone-Rolling Form

1. Plug in your waffle cone maker and turn on.
2. When the waffle cone maker is ready, usually a green light shines, spray the plates with nonstick spray for the first cone only.
3. Drop a tablespoon-sized dollop of batter on the center of the plate.
4. Close the lid and snap shut.
5. Set your timer for 100 seconds.
6. Unsnap the lid and pick up the disk and shape.
7. You have a few choices on how you would like to shape them. You may want to wear some gloves as you need to shape them right out of the cone maker or oven.

Roll cookie around a cone-rolling form. Be really careful to pinch the end or you will wind up with a cone with a hole in the end. If you have a hole it can happily be patched with a drop of melted chocolate. You can also dip cone edges in melted chocolate and then into colorful sprinkles for an extra special treat.

ice cream cones

Making Cups

Pretty fluted cups are made by placing the cookie disk on an inverted custard dish or measuring cup and pressing down with the palm of your hand or another cup that is just slightly larger. Gather folds or flare with hands if desired.

Making Fortune Cookies

Fortune cookies are super fun! Have your fortunes ready and place one in the center of your cookie disk. Fold in half like a taco and then with your thumb press an indent in the middle of the bottom of the taco so both sides fold out. Place the cookie in a muffin tin to help it hold its shape.

Using Your Oven to Prepare the Cones, Cups & Fortune Cookies.

1. Preheat oven to 350 degrees. Line three 18 by 13-inch cookie sheets with parchment paper. Make a 4-inch circle template out of a thick piece of paper or plastic lid.
2. Place template on your parchment. Spread a tablespoon of batter in center of template and smooth out with an offset spatula. Remove template and make 4 more. Each cookie sheet holds 5 disks.
3. Bake for 10-12 minutes or until golden brown.
4. Shape the cookies immediately into cones, cups, or fortune cookies

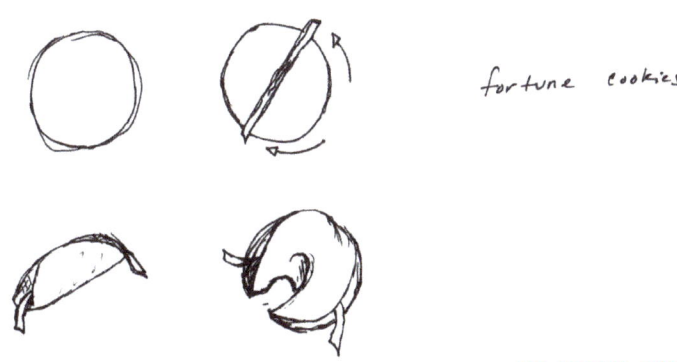

Confections

Confections

Chocolate Peanut Clusters

Aztec Truffles

Lollipops

Rocky Road Candy

Almond Brittle

Pâte de Fruit

Chocolate Peanut Clusters

Every February I pack up my tools and head to my friend Margarita Dreyer's fourth grade class where her students and I stir up big batches of these peanut clusters. They love sprinkling the candies with valentine sprinkles and giving them to their families at the end of the school day.

MAKES 25-28 CANDIES

Ingredients

12 ounces semisweet chocolate finely chopped, or chocolate chips

3 cups (1 pound) peanuts toasted and lightly salted

Garnish

2 tablespoons holiday sprinkles (optional)

1. Place parchment paper or waxed paper on 2 cookie sheets and set aside.
2. Take a 4-quart saucepan and fill it with two inches of water. Bring to a boil. Then remove it from heat.
3. Place chocolate in a medium-sized heatproof bowl and place over hot water.
4. Stir the chocolate, with a spatula, until 2/3 melted. Carefully remove the bowl from your heat source. Place the bowl on your countertop. Stir to completely melt the chocolate.
5. Stir in the nuts.
6. Scoop out heaping tablespoons of chocolate onto your prepared pans. Shake sprinkles over clusters if desired. Chill for 15 minutes to set.
7. Place clusters in festive paper muffin cups to give away or keep in a tightly enclosed container in the refrigerator for up to a week. Because this is a very quick recipe and the chocolate is not tempered, the clusters crystalize (the chocolate gets crumbly) after a day if kept at room temperature, but still taste fine.

Variations

Replace some of the peanuts with crisped rice, crystalized ginger, coconut, or dried fruit.

Aztec Truffles

Classic flavors of vanilla, chili, and cinnamon perfume this silky smooth chocolate confection.

MAKES 35 SMALL TRUFFLES

Ingredients

11 ounces semisweet or bittersweet chocolate, finely chopped
3 tablespoons (1 ½ ounces) butter, room temperature
8 ounces heavy cream
1/4 teaspoon vanilla
1/4 teaspoon chipotle or chili powder
1/2 teaspoon cinnamon

Garnish

1/2 cup cocoa powder, sifted
Or 3/4 cup turbinado sugar or granulated sugar

1. Spray the bottom of a 7 by 5-inch rectangular pan with pan spray and line the bottom and sides with plastic wrap. Make sure the plastic wrap hangs over the sides by 2-inches. Set pan aside.
2. Place chocolate and butter in a heat proof bowl.
3. Bring cream, vanilla, and spices to a simmer in a 1-quart saucepan.
4. Pour cream over the chocolate and butter and let it rest for 5 minutes before gently stirring with a spatula. Stir until the mixture is smooth and glossy. It will thicken slightly. Then pour through a sieve into prepared pan and let harden at room temperature, or overnight. You can speed up the hardening process by refrigerating the truffle filling for at least 4 hours.
5. When ready to finish, remove truffle filling from the pan by lifting up on the plastic wrap. I like to put on disposable gloves at this stage, because the chocolate may melt in your hands if your kitchen is warm. Cut truffles into 1 by 1-inch squares.
6. Roll truffles into balls or keep in square shape and roll into sifted cocoa powder or turbinado sugar.
7. Place truffles in festive paper candy cups to give away or store the truffles in a covered container, with extra cocoa powder, or sugar in the refrigerator. Let them sit at room temperature for 5 minutes to soften before eating.

Lollipops

Kids of all ages love lollipops!

MAKES 24

Ingredients

3 cups sugar
3/4 cup corn syrup
1/4 cup water
Gel paste color, a couple drops
Oil flavorings for candy, 1 teaspoon, available at kitchen and craft stores

Garnish

Holiday sprinkles

1. Spray lollipop molds, foil, or marble slab with vegetable spray (not too much or candy tastes greasy).
2. Place lollipop sticks in molds, on foil or marble slab.
3. In a 2-quart saucepan, combine the sugar, corn syrup, and water.
4. Place saucepan on high heat and stir constantly until sugar dissolves.
5. Wash down the sides of the pan with a wet brush and place a lid on the mixture for 4 minutes. Carefully remove the lid, attach a candy thermometer to the side of the pan, and bring mixture to 306 degrees without stirring.
6. Carefully remove thermometer and let the sugar syrup rest for 20 seconds (resting helps the bubbles subside). Add the color and flavor and pour the mixture carefully into the molds.
7. At this time sprinkle on any garnishes: holiday sprinkles, cocoa nibs, or glitter.

   If the candy syrup gets thick while pouring into the molds, gently reheat, but it may alter the color and flavors.
9. When candy is cool (5 minutes or so) remove from the molds and wrap individually. Lollipops keep for 2 weeks in a tightly enclosed container

Rocky Road Candy

Making candy for gifts is easy with this recipe!

MAKES 36 PIECES

Ingredients

18 ounces of semisweet chocolate, finely chopped
5 cups mini marshmallows
1 ½ cups walnuts, chopped

Garnish

2 tablespoons holiday sprinkles (optional)

Variations

Substitute dried fruit for the nuts. Try white chocolate or milk chocolate instead of semisweet. Substitute almonds or other nuts for the walnuts.

1. Place parchment paper or wax paper on a cookie sheet and set aside.
2. Fill a 4-quart saucepan with 2-inches of water. Bring to a boil. Then remove from heat.
3. Place chocolate in a medium-sized heatproof bowl and place over hot water.
4. Stir the chocolate, with a spatula, until 2/3 melted. Carefully remove the bowl from the heat source. Place the bowl on countertop. Stir to completely melt the chocolate.
5. Add nuts to the melted chocolate and stir until coated. Add marshmallows and stir until coated with chocolate.
6. Pour candy onto parchment paper and flatten with the spatula into a 12 by 12-inch square.
7. Shake sprinkles over candy if desired. Chill for 15 minutes to set. Cut into 2 by 2-inch squares. Place candy in festive paper muffin cups and give away or keep in a tightly enclosed container in the refrigerator for up to a week. Because this is a very quick recipe and the chocolate is not tempered, the chocolate crystalizes (the chocolate gets crumbly) after a day if kept at room temperature, but still taste fine.

Almond Brittle

It's fun to watch the students crunching on this golden confection, as they pack up treats to drop by friends' houses on the way home from class.

MAKES ONE COOKIE SHEET

Ingredients

14 ounces (2 cups) granulated sugar
2 ounces (1/4 cup) water
10 ½ ounces (1 cup) corn syrup
1 pound (4 cups) almonds, slivered, warm
1 teaspoon salt
1 ounce (2 tablespoons) butter, softened
2 teaspoons vanilla
1 ½ teaspoons baking soda

1. Oil the bottom and sides of a cookie sheet. Oil an offset spatula. Set both aside.
2. In a 4-quart saucepan combine the sugar, water, and corn syrup. Place over a moderately high heat and bring to a boil stirring constantly until sugar dissolves. Brush down the sides with a wet pastry brush then cover and cook for 4 minutes.
3. Remove the cover and clip on a candy thermometer. Let the mixture heat to 240 degrees, without stirring.
4. Add the almonds and stir the mixture until it reaches 311 degrees. Carefully watch the last 10 degrees as the temperature rises dramatically towards the end of the cooking time.
5. Remove pot from the heat and add the salt, butter, vanilla, and baking soda. Stir to combine. The baking soda will darken the color of the brittle and lighten the texture.
6. Pour the mixture onto the greased baking pan. Smooth with the greased spatula. Cool to room temperature. Break into pieces.
7. Store candy at room temperature for one week in a tightly enclosed container.

Pâte de Fruit

I'm a fan of fruity chewy candy and the French have designed the perfect fruit chew confection called pâte de fruit, which translates to fruit paste. A pretty dish of these gems delight friends at winter holiday parties.

MAKES 36 CANDIES

Ingredients

1 cup raspberry puree *
2 tablespoons sugar
2 teaspoons pectin
1 cup sugar
1/4 cup corn syrup
1/2 teaspoon citric acid **
Coarse sugar, super fine sugar or granulated sugar for dusting.

* Look for fruit puree in your frozen foods section of your grocery store or make your own.

** Citric acid is available at most kitchen and craft stores.

1. Line a 6 by 6-inch square pan with plastic wrap and set aside.
2. In a small bowl combine the 2 tablespoons sugar with the pectin. Set aside
3. Pour the raspberry puree in a small saucepan and bring to a simmer whisking constantly.
4. Add the pectin and sugar mixture and whisk to combine.
5. Add the remaining 1 cup of sugar and bring to a boil.
6. Add the corn syrup and bring the mixture back to a boil. Attach a candy thermometer to the side of your pan. Continue whisking and boiling until the temperature reaches 225 degrees.
7. Remove from heat. Add citric acid. Pour into prepared pan.
8. Keep the Pâte de fruit at room temperature. It should set within 1-2 hours.
9. Sprinkle sugar onto a piece of parchment paper and invert candy onto the sugar.
10. Dust with more sugar and slice into shapes with an oiled knife, pizza cutter, or caramel cutter.

In memory of my father John William Fordham, who helped me sell my first cakes when I was five and inspired my professional dreams with his favorite phrase: Keep a PMA—Positive Mental Attitude.

ACKNOWLEDGEMENTS

This book has been in the making for 10 years, in my mind anyway. There were many wonderful people who helped me to finally put my thoughts and recipes on paper.

I could not have completed this project without my husband Matt. My most enthusiastic cheerleader, who eagerly took up his pen to help craft my words, and helped test recipes including a three-day scone-a-thon.

An immense amount of gratitude goes out to my sister Mary Fordham Kuckens for illustrating the recipes with such skill and loving care.

For my mom, Marilyn Fordham, whose creative cooking influenced me to continue on with the craft professionally and who has been a joyful supporter during the writing process.

Richard Army, for all those times sitting around our tables hashing out ideas and giving me a great start editing the book.

Catherine Peters-Graham for never shying away every time I brought out my manuscript, in much need of her copy editing expertise.

My son Dana for his recipe testing skills, enthusiasm every step of the way and for his filming expertise in creating my online videos.

My daughter Jeanne for her supreme editing skills, artistic expertise in illustrating the diagrams, and for her sense of humor during what seemed like an endless editing process.

Sylvie-Marie Drescher, at Bookshop Santa Cruz for her artistic support and publishing expertise.

Appreciation also to the many friends and family who cheered me on, tested recipes, and shared information:

Mary Fordham Kuckens, Jeanne Peterson, Sarita Fordham Aguilar, Jane Fordham Garcia, Henry Kuckens, Kim Cunningham, Margarita Dreyer, Tamara Wright, Robin Ellis, Linda Guy, Sally Klein, Patti Le Day, Jocelyn O'Morris, Jill Gallo and Scott Johnson and their wonderful staff at the Cabrillo College Extension office, and the ever smiling Cliff Hall and his very helpful staff.

Index

A

Almond Brittle, 109
Apricot Galette, 87
Appetizers, 1-11
    Cherry Tomato Crostini, 11
    Inari Sushi, 8
    Fresh Berry Salsa, 4
    Herb and Cheese Cream Scones, 10
    Mini Vegetable Quiche, 9
    Parmesan Cheese Straws, 6
    Pesto Cheese Torta, 3
    Rice Paper Wraps, 7
    Salami Pinwheels, 5
    Salsa Fresca, 4
Apples
    Apple Coffee Cake, 15
    Apple Galette, 87
    Apple Spice Cake with Cream Cheese Icing, 77
    Apple Pocket Pies, 62
    Matt's Apple Crisp, 60
Aztec Truffles, 106

B

Bacon and Cheese Scones, 18
Bananas
    Chocolate Banana Strudel, 21
    Gluten-Free Banana Coffee Cake, 16

Basil
- Cheesy Pesto Tart, 47
- Lemon Basil Pasta, 42
- Pesto Cheese Torta, 3
- Tomato Basil Galette, 53

Black Bean Chili Con Carne, 54

Black Bean Soup, 27

Blackberry Galette, 87

Bountiful Jam Squares, 72

Breakfast, 13-23
- Apple Coffee Cake, 15
- Bacon and Cheese Scones, 18
- Chocolate Banana Strudel, 21
- Chocolate Scones, 19
- Gluten-Free Banana Coffee Cake, 16
- Gluten-Free Pumpkin Coffee Cake, 17
- Green Smoothie, 23
- Hearty Steel Cut Oatmeal, 22
- Henny Penny Egg, 20

C

Cacao Nib Butter Cookies, 68

Cakes
- Apple Spice Cake with Cream Cheese Icing, 77
- Glamorous French Chocolate Cake, 79
- Jeanne's Strawberry Shortcake, 80
- Simple Plum Cake, 78

Cantuccini, 71

Cassoulet Soup, 32

Cheesy Pesto Tart, 47

Cherry Tomato Crostini, 11

Chicken Molé, 51

Chocolate
- Aztec Truffles, 106

Cacao Nib Butter cookies , 68
Chicken Molé, 51
Chocolate Banana Strudel, 21
Chocolate Peanut Clusters, 105
Chocolate Sauce, 98
Chocolate Scones, 19
Chocolate Walnut Tart, 90
Cocoa Carne Asada, 48
Glamorous French Chocolate Cake, 79
Rocky Road Candy, 108

Cinnamon Whipped Cream, 89

Coconut Rice, 35

Confections, 103-110

Almond Brittle, 109
Aztec Truffles, 106
Chocolate Peanut Clusters, 105
Lollipops, 107
Pâte de Fruit, 110
Rocky Road Candy, 108

Cookies, 65-71

Bountiful Jam Squares, 72
Cacao Nib Butter Cookies, 68
Cantuccini, 71
Fortune Cookies, 100
Gluten-Free Bountiful Jam Squares, 73
Gluten-Free Flour Blend, 71
Meyer Lemon Refrigerator Cookies, 67
Oatmeal Cookies, 70
Peanut Butter Gems, 69

Cornbread with Honey Butter, 44

Couscous, 36

Cream Cheese Icing, 77

Cream of Broccoli Soup, 28

D

Dana's Blueberry Buckle, 63

Desserts, 57-63
    Apple Pocket Pies, 62
    Dana's Blueberry Buckle, 63
    Matt's Apple Crisp, 60
    Plum Crisp, 59
    Strawberry Rhubarb Cobbler, 61

E

Entrees, 45-55
    Black Bean Chili con Carne, 54
    Cheesy Pesto Tart, 47
    Chicken Molé, 51
    Cocoa Carne Asada, 48
    Salmon Sliders with Wasabi Mayonnaise, 50
    Sushi, 55
    Teriyaki Salmon, 49
    Tomato Basil Galette, 53

F

Fish
    Salmon Sliders, 50
    Sushi, 55
    Teriyaki Salmon, 49

Fortune Cookies, 100
Fresh Berry Salsa, 4
Fresh Fruit Tart, 91
Fresh Strawberry Sorbet

G

Galettes and Tarts, 83-91
    Galette pastry Dough, 85

    Tart Dough, 90
    Chocolate Walnut Tart, 90
    Fresh Fruit Tart, 91
    Fruit Galette Variations, 87
    Pumpkin Chiffon Tart, 88
    Southern Pecan Tart with Cinnamon Whipped Cream, 89
    Streusel Topping, 86
    Very Berry Galette, 86

Garden Fresh Tomato Soup, 29

Garlic Mashed Potatoes, 37

Glamorous French Chocolate Cake, 79

Gluten-Free Baking

    Gluten-Free Flour Blend, 71
    Corn Bread with Honey Butter, 44
    Glamorous French Chocolate Cake, 79
    Gluten-Free Bountiful Jam Squares, 73
    Gluten-Free Banana Coffee Cake, 16
    Gluten-Free Pumpkin Coffee Cake, 17
    Peanut Butter Gems, 69

Green Smoothie, 23

H

Hearty Steel Cut Oatmeal, 22

Henny Penny Egg, 20

Herb and Cheese Cream Scones, 10

Honey Butter, 44

I

Ice Cream, 95-96

Ice Cream Cones, Cups, and Fortune Cookies, 93-100

    Mexican Chocolate Ice Cream, 96
    Vanilla Ice Cream, 84

Inari Sushi, 8
Italian Sausage Soup, 30

J

Jam

    Bountiful Jam Squares, 72
    Gluten-Free Bountiful Jam Squares, 73

Jeanne's Strawberry Shortcake, 80

L

Leek and Potato Soup, 31
Lemon Basil Pasta, 42
Lollipops, 107

M

Matt's Apple Crisp, 60
Mexican Chocolate Ice Cream, 96
Meyer Lemon Refrigerator Cookies, 67

N

Nectarine Galette, 87

O

Oatmeal Cookies, 70

P

Parmesan Cheese Straws, 6
Pasta Alfredo, 41

Pâte de Fruit, 110
Peanut Butter Gems, 69
Pear Galette, 87
Polenta, 38

Plums
- Plum Crisp, 59
- Plum Galette, 87
- Simple Plum Cake, 78

Pumpkin
- Gluten-Free Pumpkin Coffee Cake, 17
- Pumpkin Chiffon Tart, 88

Q

Quinoa, 43

R

Rocky Road Candy, 108
Rice Paper Wraps, 7

S

Salami Pinwheels, 5
Salmon Sliders with Wasabi Mayonnaise, 50

Sauces
- Caramel Sauce, 99
- Chocolate Sauce, 98

Scones
- Bacon and Cheese Scones 18
- Chocolate Scones, 19
- Herb and Cheese Cream Scones, 10

Side Dishes, 33-44
- Coconut Rice, 35

- Corn Bread with Honey Butter, 44
- Couscous, 36
- Garlic Mashed Potatoes, 37
- Lemon Basil Pasta, 42
- Pasta Alfredo, 41
- Polenta, 38
- Quinoa, 43
- Summer Gratin, 40
- Tian, 39

Simple Plum Cake, 78

Sorbet

- Fresh Strawberry Sorbet, 97

Southern Pecan Tart with Cinnamon Whipped Cream, 89

Strawberries

- Fresh Strawberry Sorbet, 97
- Jeanne's Strawberry Shortcake, 80
- Strawberry Rhubarb Cobbler, 61

Streusel Topping, 89
Summer Gratin, 40
Sushi, 55

T

Tart Dough, 90
Tomato Basil Galette, 53
Teriyaki Salmon, 49
Tian, 39

V

Vanilla Ice Cream, 95
Vegetable Mini Quiche, 9
Very Berry Galette, 86

W

Wasabi Mayonnaise, 50

www.ingramcontent.com/pod-product-compliance
Lightning Source LLC
Chambersburg PA
CBHW040750020526
44118CB00042B/2853